Attack your enemy in the places they cannot defend.

Sun Tze 500 BC

LOW CARB
MADE EASY

Weight loss • Diabetes • Heart Disease • Cholesterol
Chronic Fatigue • Sugar Addiction • Polycystic Ovarian Syndrome

JOHN RATCLIFFE Dip TCM, Grad Dip Psy

and

CHERIE VAN STYN BN

HINKLER
BOOKS

Low Carb Made Easy
Published in 2003 by Hinkler Books Pty Ltd
17–23 Redwood Drive
Dingley VIC 3172 Australia
www.hinklerbooks.com

Previously published by Better Healing Press in November 1998
Revised May 2002

Reprinted 2004 (four times)

© Text 1998 John Ratcliffe
© Cover Design 2003 Hinkler Books Pty Ltd

ISBN 1741 211 646

Cover Design: Silvana Paolini
Typesetting: Midland Typesetters, Maryborough, Victoria
Printed and bound in Australia

This book is intended as a reference guide only. The information presented here is
designed to help you make informed choices about your health. It is not intended as
a substitute for any treatment or weight loss program prescribed by your doctor.

'To all my patients, without whom I would never have developed this knowledge and understanding.'

Acknowledgments

I would like to thank my partner Cherie Van Styn who convinced me to keep writing after the computer crashed and I lost the original book entirely. Cherie contributed selflessly to the development of the recipes and was very patient when experimenting on me with the various dishes.

I would also like to thank Karin Serry, who is not only a great friend but was the first person to make me aware of this information.

And finally to the many patients who took my advice and followed this way of eating, lost lots of weight, and had to buy new clothes.

TOLD YOU SO!

Contents

Introduction   9

PART 1: The Explanation   **15**
Chapter 1: Blood Sugar, Insulin and Weight Loss   17
Chapter 2: Carbohydrate Categories   33
Chapter 3: Compelling Reasons   57
Chapter 4: Getting Good Results   73

PART 2: The Food   **79**
Chapter 5: The 7 Day Meal Planner   81
Chapter 6: The Recipes   89

PART 3: Now What?   **253**
Chapter 7: Frequently Asked Questions   255
Chapter 8: What Do I Do Now I Have
      Lost the Weight?   265

Conclusion   271

Tables and Appendices   **273**
Appendix A: GI tables   274
Appendix B: Glycemic Loading   286
Appendix C: Metabolic Syndrome   289
Appendix D: Glossary   290
Appendix E: Conversion Table   291
Bibliography and further reading   292
The Glycemic Index Elsewhere on the Internet   295
Recipe Index   297
Index   302

Introduction

For those who came in late, this is the third edition of the book we first published in November 1998, titled *Sugar Science*. In response to the requests for more recipes, my partner Cherie Van Styn released a companion book, *The Low-carbohydrate Gourmet Cookbook*, in early 2000. Due to the popularity of the two books both in Australia and overseas, we decided to put them into one title, add some things and give it the more accurate description of *Low Carb Made Easy*.

How did something that originally began life as a collection of notes for my patients eventually come to be a book enjoyed by so many and translated into three languages? Well, it's all because I have been helping people with low-carb diets since 1995. Back then, few people knew anything about controlling blood sugar levels, especially when it came to weight loss.

I practise medicine for a living and I see people for all sorts of reasons. I can fix your back, help you have kids, clear up your skin and tell you what to do about your relationship. You name it, I've treated it. The funny thing is, it is unusual for me to be unable to help someone. Why? Because I'm not a regular doctor.

I was trained for nine years by a very senior Chinese Professor. So after a few years of studying the basics of Western medicine, I continued with Traditional Chinese Medicine (TCM) to eventually become a TCM practitioner, or as I put it, a 'Chinese Doctor'. It may sound absurd but there you have it.

Now I can appreciate that you're probably not interested in me or TCM, but understanding some of its principles may not be wasted when it comes to understanding this book. TCM treats the causes and not just the symptoms. Preventing illness is much better than cure. TCM has a unique quality very different from its Western counterpart.

For all of my adult life I have been involved in medicine. I have treated thousands and thousands of people. But there had always been one persistent problem that has caused both Chinese and Western medicine great difficulty – how to help people with their weight.

When overweight patients came to me for help, all I could tell them was 'eat less and exercise more', but deep down we both knew that there had to be a better way. So in 1993, I set out to try to find it.

Luckily it wasn't too long before the answer came to me in the form of a letter. One of my patients had a girlfriend overseas who had written to her. She presented the letter to me saying, 'I don't understand what she's trying to tell me, but you will, when you understand, then you can explain it to me'.

From my training in the '80s, I could only vaguely recollect that insulin was responsible for fat absorption, but this was the very first time I'd read about the glycemic index (GI). When something new comes along and I think it's worthwhile, I like to try it myself. Before long, I was a stone lighter and my patient was knocking back marriage proposals. The rest, shall we say, was history.

So what is the GI all about? As I mentioned, according to my text books, the relationship between insulin and fat was already known. The reason why I hadn't heard about low-carb sooner was that no-one really knew how to control blood sugar levels effectively with diet. As a result, there was no information.

The people who really needed this knowledge the most were, of course, diabetics. Dieticians and nutritionists had, for years, been telling them what to eat and what not to eat based on laboratory analysis. Unfortunately, in spite of all the research, it wasn't solving their fluctuating blood sugar level problems. So the most well-funded organization, The Diabetics Association of America, decided to do its own research. It was very straightforward and surprising that no-one had thought of it any sooner.

What they did was actually *eat* the food and then measure their blood sugar levels. If there is one thing that diabetics know about, it's pricking the finger and measuring blood sugar levels and it wasn't long before they realised that a lot of the food they'd been told would have no effect on their blood sugar levels was actually doing the exact opposite. There were enormous swings when there weren't supposed to be any. That's basically how the GI began.

Now, as one can imagine, the Diabetics Association was pretty happy with all this but they weren't trying to save the world; they only wanted to know what to eat. As a result, no one seemed to be aware at the time that the discovery was going to have far-reaching consequences beyond diabetes.

That was in the late 1970s when we all had more hair and bigger lapels. It took another fifteen years for that knowledge to arrive at my office in Melbourne, Australia. That, I might add, is just the way it goes when it comes to medicine. New discoveries take ages to get recognition. First they're ridiculed, then attacked, then slowly gain acceptance and then become doctrine.

When *I* first realised that there was a way of controlling blood sugar levels, I knew in a heart beat that this was going to change quite a few things. Elevated or fluctuating blood sugar levels were responsible for many diseases, including obesity.

So after a little trial and error, I developed a formula for following a low-carb diet that I knew worked. The next step was getting other people to use it and it wasn't long before they were also getting great results.

When it comes to eating healthily, it is no surprise that people get confused. Every women's magazine, for at least as long as I can remember, has included something about dieting. TV, radio and print often give conflicting and confusing advice when it comes to this. Sometimes it's reducing calories, others times it's low-fat or only eating at certain times or grazing. Then it's the Israeli Army diet, then it's the soup diet, then it's Pritikin, then it's the raw food diet! Take it from me, the LAST thing the world needs now is another diet.

The information contained in this book equips you with a very easy way to lose weight and look after your health. Naturally, weight loss need not be your only motivation. Many patients with cholesterol problems, diabetes, hypoglycaemia, sugar addiction and polycystic ovarian syndrome have had great results using the formula

Low carb is certainly a revolution. I have followed it from the beginning, as have many thousands of my patients and readers, and a great many of them are very happy for having done so. Every now and again, an apparent stranger arrives at the clinic saying, 'Remember me?' We look at them for a while before saying, 'Oh! You came and got a copy of the book.' The person usually beams, places their hands on their hips and parades around, showing off their new figure. Who knows, after reading the book, there's no reason why you might not end up doing the same!

For many years I have sat and explained the GI to people. Individually, one on one, face to face. Occasionally I will address an audience, be it on the radio, in person etc. Not surprisingly, I have become very used to explaining it in a way that people can understand.

I wrote the book in the same way as I like to explain it, so you should find it easy to read, easy to understand and easy to apply. Certainly, there are some very complex explanations behind the hows and whys, but I have *deliberately* avoided making it more difficult than it has to be. Go to the references at the back of the book if you want to learn more.

Once you understand the basic concepts, then it is straightforward from there and it won't be long before you have mastery over this information. Make mastery your goal. The better you are at using this information, the better the results will be.

To help you get started, Chérie has written a comprehensive meal planner and included some 130 low-carb recipes. To tell you the truth, I had no idea what an excellent cook Chérie was before we started working on the recipes. Having the honour of being the test pilot for most of them, I can honestly say that 'mind blowing', was an expression often used.

As if that's not enough, we have also set up a web site which offers support, new recipes, many answers to questions and even the opportunity to communicate with other enthusiasts. It can be found at www.low-carbohydrate.com.

I know that *Low Carb Made Easy* will help you in many ways and quite possibly create a new direction in you health and lifestyle for the future. It is my sincere hope that the information contained in these pages will become as much a part of your life as it has for my patients and me.

John Ratcliffe
Melbourne, 2003.

PART I

The Explanation

CHAPTER I

Blood Sugar, Insulin and Weight Loss

Today, people are eating less meat, fat, eggs and dairy than ever before. In spite of this, people are, on average, heavier than ever before and the trend is increasing at an alarming rate. The World Heath Organisation (WHO) announced last year that the number of obese people now equalled the number of starving in the Third World.

Coincidentally, a recent study revealed that sugar consumption in the Western world has risen from a modest 2.25 kg per year in the 1800s to a staggering 80 kg. That's a 4000% increase! It begs the question, 'What must this be doing to our health?'

Obesity, diabetes, and heart disease are on the increase both in my country, Australia, as well as the USA. However, it's also increasing in just about any other country that follows Western dietary habits.

At the moment there is a glut of sugar on the world market and it's no surprise that it has found its way into almost every food. When you go to the supermarket, try finding something, off the shelf, that does not list sugar as an ingredient. It's almost impossible.

We know that sugar is an addictive substance and, not surprisingly, food producers have also known this. Add a little to your product and people will be wanting more. These days we use the term 'sugar addiction' often. People can get 'hooked' on it like a narcotic, and go through withdrawals without it. From my experience of helping people get over this, one can say that the bigger the exposure to sugar, the bigger the withdrawal can be.

What follows is a unifying explanation as to why you may have had trouble losing weight and keeping it off. It also offers some insight into other health problems such as diabetes, heart disease and polycystic ovarian syndrome. Like every good story it's all in the telling, so first we'll start by getting to know the cast of 'players' namely: carbohydrate, protein, fat, blood sugar and insulin.

Carbohydrate, our main character, is basically stored energy. Some examples of carbohydrates are fruits, vegetables, grains, legumes, cereals, lollies, biscuits and cakes. Some types of carbohydrate are called starches, whilst others are called sugars. Regardless, the body converts all carbohydrates into fuel, and that fuel is called glucose.

Protein is our second character. It is often referred to as the building block of the body. Protein is used to make things like muscle, hormones, blood and a few chemicals. Most proteins come from animal products like dairy, meat, poultry and seafood. There are some vegetables that also contain proteins, but they are a form of protein that the body uses poorly. Although vegetarians would like to think otherwise, it is irrefutable that the body gets far more mileage from, and prefers, first class proteins derived from animals and seafood.

Fats is the third character in our story. Also known as lipids, these include oils (such as vegetable oil), butter and animal fats. Animal fats are the fat you might trim off meat before eating it. These fats are the reserves that the *animal* has put into storage for later use.

The last two characters that you need to be familiar with are **blood sugar level** and **insulin**. Blood sugar refers to the amount of glucose that is in the blood at any one time. The glucose in our blood is the type of sugar the body uses for fuel. It is transported around in the blood stream to reach all the cells. Once inside the cells, glucose is used as fuel to produce energy.

Normally there is about one gram of glucose per litre of blood. Not much really when you consider that the adult body contains only 5½ litres of blood. The level of glucose in our blood is called the Blood Sugar Level or BSL for short.

Insulin, our last cast member, is a hormone that is produced by the pancreas. Place your hand on the area above your belly button and this is roughly the position of your pancreas. The pancreas releases insulin to control the level of sugar in the blood. When we eat carbohydrates they are broken down by the digestive system into glucose and absorbed into the blood stream, causing a rise in the blood sugar levels. If the blood sugar level rises above a certain limit, insulin will be released by the pancreas. This maintains the amount of sugar in the blood at a healthy level. Too little and you lapse into a coma, too much and you go blind and die.

Later in our story, we can find out how insulin controls the blood sugar levels and where the excess sugar goes. But that's it until then, and, like all good stories, some suspense!

Now we have familiarised ourselves with the list of characters: carbohydrate, protein, fat, blood sugar and insulin. All have specific functions in the body and all have a special relationship to each other. The stage is set, the house lights dim, let's get on with the story!

Scene 1: The Story Unfolds

Enter the main character, carbohydrate. Carbohydrate is a collective term covering the different forms of sugar that can be broken down to provide energy in the body. Most people are familiar with the terms 'complex carbohydrate' and 'simple carbohydrate'. These two terms refer to the *density* of the carbohydrate. For example, take a complex carbohydrate like a potato. A potato is densely packed with lots of glucose forming its structure, all tightly squeezed together. Hence the term *complex*. It was believed, that for the body to absorb the glucose, it would take a long time to dismantle it, so it would to be broken down and absorbed slowly. Simple carbohydrates, on the other hand, were believed to be broken down quickly for the body to use as fuel. A simple carbohydrate, like a lolly, could be broken down and absorbed quickly.

Again I remind you that when referring to carbohydrates, whether simple or complex, we are still talking about sugar.

The Glycemic Index

As previously mentioned, the Glycemic Index (or GI) is a scale that was developed in the early '80s, to help diabetics control their BSL. The GI was found by determining how much glucose different carbohydrates produced when eaten. Before the GI, diabetics were trying to follow their doctor's advice by eating more complex carbohydrates and less simple sugars.

They believed that complex carbohydrates, being so densely packed, would break down slowly, and therefore the rise in the blood sugar would be gradual. This was the view for many years, but unfortunately it was never tested. As a result, controlling the blood sugar levels continued to be a problem, and no one could really understand why.

Diabetes is a disease that occurs when the pancreas

does not produce enough insulin to control the person's blood sugar levels. Unless treated, the person's blood sugar levels will rise too high. A high blood sugar level above the normal level can cause serious health problems.

As I described earlier, the breakthrough came when a group of people sat down, ate a variety of different carbohydrates and measured their BSL at fifteen minute intervals. Some of the people had diabetes and others didn't.

From the results, a scale was created ranking the different types of foods according to the rise in the blood sugar levels of the volunteers. Glucose was given an arbitrary value of 100. Since glucose is the type of sugar the body breaks the carbohydrates down to, all the results for the different carbohydrates/foods were *indexed* to this. We now refer to the resulting tables as the Glycemic Index (GI). Carbohydrates that produce a lot of glucose and raise the blood sugar levels significantly have a high GI and those that have little effect on blood sugar levels have a low GI. That's where we get the term 'low carb diet' because it actually means 'a diet, using carbohydrates that have a low GI', and not a diet low in carbs as some will try and have you believe.

The GI revealed how much of an effect a particular carbohydrate would have on the blood sugar levels when eaten. The GI also gave some unexpected insight into previously held concepts of complex and simple carbohydrates.

Complex carbohydrates, had long been thought to break down at a slower rate than simple carbohydrates. It was believed that if you ate a more complex carbohydrate, the body would take more time to digest and absorb its densleypacked structure. It was imagined that a gradual rise in the blood sugar level would result and the body would then have a more constant supply of glucose to burn up. Hence the practice by athletes of loading up on complex carbohydrates before an endurance event. It was also believed that if you wanted a sudden burst of energy, it was better to eat a simple carbohydrate like a barley sugar, because it would break down rapidly and provide instant energy.

With the discovery of the GI, it was patently obvious that the ideas about complex and simple carbohydrates were flawed. What the study revealed was that the body converted the sugars in complex carbohydrates into glucose at the same rate as simple carbohydrates. The BSL of volunteers who had eaten a tablespoon of glucose, rose and fell over the same time period as those who had eaten a potato. Whether the carbohydrates were complex or simple didn't seem to matter. The researchers now knew why diabetics had trouble controlling their BSL's, despite the best advice at the time. Great news!

Scene 2: The Return of Insulin

Here we return to our friend insulin. Remember that it has the job of lowering blood sugar levels to maintain the level of glucose in the blood? Insulin's unique way of doing this is the thing which should interest us all.

To do this, it first converts the glucose into sort of a glucose syrup called glycogen, which is stored in the liver. This acts like an energy reserve that can be quickly converted back into glucose if required. However, the liver can only store so much and if the blood sugar levels continue to rise, then the excess glycogen goes on to be metabolised by insulin into fat.

This is why a proportion of the fat stored around your body is the product of excess sugars in your diet that have metabolised, first to glucose, then to glycogen and finally to fat. This fat can be converted back to fuel for energy if the glucose and glycogen has been depleted, but the idea is, that in times of plenty the body creates reserves to protect you in times of famine.

This is an excellent built-in feature and anyone who has seen the Reality TV series 'Survivor,' for example, can see that when everyday people are placed in a situation where food is scarce, they can survive without too much trouble for quite a while, sure they get really skinny and wander around in a daze but they 'survive'.

This ability comes along with our earliest evolution. But unless you are actually lost in the wilderness, or doing it for a million dollars or are in the middle of a famine then the chances are that you will never ever need it.

Although society has changed dramatically in the past fifty thousand years, our bodies haven't and when given the chance, will never pass up an opportunity to store more energy. Happy in the thought of the great job it's doing and mindful of how lucky you are that you never seem to run out of food.

When we eat something that is high in energy, like a candy bar for example, you'll get a rise in your blood sugar levels and feel a lift, but that's not the end of it. The *excess* energy isn't wasted. How does your body know that wasn't the last candy bar for the next few months? So to be on the safe side, it takes what's left over from the 5½ grams of glucose that's floating around in the blood, and the rest goes into reserve.

The body is looking out for our best interests, but one needs to understand that there is no limit to how much energy it can actually put away! As we see with obesity, the more you give it, the more it saves. The body will continue to save up more and more reserves. Occasionally, the news will have pictures of an extremely obese person who has grown so big they can't move any more and are now being lifted by a crane out of their house!

So back to the source. Where does all this stored energy come from? You may have already guessed that carbohydrates have a big role. Eating carbohydrates that have a high GI raises your blood sugar levels higher than normal. This rise causes insulin to be released by the pancreas. As I pointed out earlier, eventually the insulin can actually convert the excess sugar into fat.

Farmers, for example, have known for centuries that you don't fatten animals by feeding them fat, you fatten them by feeding them grains like corn, and vegetables like potato. But no one ever stopped to consider that the same may be true for human animals. Although this should have been obvious, medical history is punctuated by many misunderstandings. Fifty years ago doctors thought smoking was good for you! So this bring us to the first piece of information to commit to memory:

'Certain carbohydrates can be fattening.'

'What are these carbohydrates?' I hear you ask. Well, it all depends on how much glucose the carbohydrate produces and how much it affects the blood sugar levels. The higher the GI, the more glucose the carbohydrate produces, the higher it raises your blood sugar levels. The surplus will then be transformed into fat. The task is to identify which carbohydrates give our bodies large amounts of glucose and which don't. In other words, which carbohydrates are good and which carbohydrates should be avoided.

At school, I learnt that glucose produced more glucose than anything else. So glucose would have to be one of the bad carbohydrates and I guess you don't have to be Werner Von Braun* to have worked that one out! Now, if you remember from Part 1 where we discussed the GI, you might have a clue to identifying a bad carbohydrate.

The GI actually tells us which carbohydrates raise our blood sugar levels and can make us put on weight. Interestingly, when we look at the GI, we can see that there are many carbohydrates that actually raise the blood sugar levels nearly as high as if we were eating straight sugar.

Next is your first look at the GI using some carbohydrates as examples. I must warn you that this may severely affect you and your future understanding about food!

Please note, just for the record, that those carbs with a GI less than 50 are considered <u>below</u> the limit at which insulin is released in most people, and should not be a problem.

---

*German rocket scientist, Father of the Apollo program.

Carbohydrate	Glycemic Index
Maltose (Beer)	110
Glucose	**100**
Parsnips	97
White bread	90
White rice	87
Potato	**85**
Honey	75
Pumpkin	75
Sugar	**72**
Pasta	70
Carrots	70
Corn flakes	70
Popcorn	70
Chocolate bar	70
Corn	70
Beetroot	65
Banana	60
Jam	55
Spaghetti	55
Whole rye bread	50
Fresh pasta	40
Beans	30
Lentils	30
Fresh fruit	30
Fructose	20
Lettuce, tomato, mushroom	15

Oh my! If you suddenly heard a thud and are looking up at the ceiling it is because you have fallen off your chair! Stop clutching your chest and pull yourself together. Remember, the higher up it is on the list, the more glucose that carbohydrate produces, and the more there is to be converted into fat. Now the sensitivity of your body to glucose can vary a little from individual to individual, but as a general rule of thumb the GI is fairly accurate.

Before you start throwing out three-quarters of your pantry, I would like to introduce you to the next part of this story. Namely the part that has the good news.

Scene 3: The Fat Lady Sings

In the previous section we discovered that carbohydrates with a high GI produce an excessive amount of glucose, and that excess is converted into fat by insulin. But, what about if we eat fat? What happens then?

Fats are absorbed in the same way as carbohydrates. This means they need to be in the presence of insulin to be placed into storage. Insulin is the substance that also allows the body to absorb the fats in the first place. So here is the second thing to remember.

'Fat can only be absorbed in the presence of insulin.'

Although fat itself is a version of stored energy, fat will not raise your blood sugar levels, and therefore, fat alone will not cause the pancreas to secrete insulin.

The only thing that will raise your blood sugar levels and put the pancreas to work, yep you guessed it, is the wrong carbohydrates.

So eating fats does not make you fat. It is actually the types of carbohydrate that you include with fats that will determine if you absorb the fat or not. Only when you combine fat with carbohydrates that raise your blood sugar levels to the point where insulin is released, will the fats be absorbed. So here is the third piece of information that you need to enshrine in your memory:

'Eating fat does not make you fat. It is the type of carbohydrates combined with fats that will make them be absorbed.'

Having understood this, it is now very easy to see why we put on weight. It soon becomes obvious that just about every meal we eat generally contains a combination of some fat, and carbohydrates that cause insulin to be released, and fat to be absorbed. When you go out to a restaurant, for example, the first thing that normally appears on the table is some bread. What's a roast without potato? At the end of a meal you have dessert and so on. With our new understanding of fats and carbohydrates, we now know that by selectively removing the carbo components that raise the blood sugar levels, we can also remove the problem of absorbing fat.

The popularity of low-fat diets is a good example of how we previously misunderstood the body's process of absorbing fat. This lack of understanding meant that the only way of trying to lose weight was to take as much fat out of the diet as possible. By using our new information we can see that it is not the fat that needs to be removed, but rather the wrong type of carbohydrates. Obviously controlling your blood sugar levels is a more effective way of taking control of your weight. Let's have an example.

Take the traditional hearty breakfast of bacon and eggs, tomato and toast. It is pretty much impossible to lose weight from eating this type of food according to present opinion. According to what we have just learnt, it is only the *toast* that makes the meal fattening, because this is the component that raises the blood sugar levels. We know that bread has a high GI from the tables on page 27. Therefore we know that the bread will raise the blood sugar levels, cause insulin to be released and any excess sugar in the blood will be eventually get converted into fat. The release of insulin will also result in any fat in the meal being absorbed as more padding for the stomach, hips and thighs and more problems for the person with high cholesterol. If by now you are starting to realise what all this means, then you can under-stand why this information is making a lot of so called 'experts' do an about-face and run for cover.

Let's go back to our example. By simply avoiding the toast, the meal is not and <u>cannot</u> be fattening. Bacon isn't a carbohydrate and neither is the egg. They are fat and protein combined together, and although the tomato is a carbo-hydrate, it has a very low glycemic index, lower than 20, meaning it has little effect on the blood sugar levels and doesn't cause insulin to be released. Therefore, when you eat bacon, eggs and tomato without toast, the blood sugar levels will not rise, insulin will not be released, and the process of fat being absorbed cannot take place. But before you order a lifetime supply of bacon and eggs you need to learn a little bit more.

As I have stated earlier, carbohydrates are the key element in your diet that will determine whether or not a meal is fattening. It is obvious to us now that, without understanding the GI, all the information on simple and complex carbohydrates is meaningless. If you can't tell which carbohydrates are going raise your blood sugar levels, then you can't control the release of insulin and it's the insulin that is at the heart of it all. Naturally Western medicine discovered how insulin worked long ago. The problem was understanding how each different type of carbohydrates affected the blood sugar levels. This is what really mattered.

As we've discussed in this first part of our story, not all carbohydrates are created equal. To fully understand this knowledge we must delve a little deeper into the GI. Let's continue.

CHAPTER 2

Carbohydrate Categories

The first category we'll look at is the carbohydrates with a high GI. They cause the blood sugar levels to shoot up, so we'll refer to them as **bad carbohydrates**. Next there are those carbohydrates that have a 'middle of the road' GI. These are the ones that have a more moderate effect on the blood sugar level. They will cause the blood sugar level to rise, but only to the point where insulin needs to be produced. If the blood sugar level goes over this limit, then only a small amount of insulin is released to bring the level back to within the normal range. We'll call these **moderate carbohydrates**. The last group is the carbohydrates that have a low GI. These are the ones that no matter how much you eat, they never produce enough glucose to cause insulin to be released. In the case of controlling your weight this is highly desirable. We shall call them **good carbohydrates**. Next is a table dividing some common carbohydrates into their respective classes.

Bad Carbohydrates	Moderate Carbohydrates	Good Carbohydrates
White or brown sugar	Whole cereals Wheat, Oats, Barley, Millet	Alfalfa sprouts
Honey		Celery
White or whole-meal flour	Bran	Bamboo shoots
	Pure Rye	Cucumber
Bread	Bread*	Tomato
Crisp Bread	Basmarti Rice*	Radish
Biscuits	Fresh Pasta*	Lettuce
Cakes	Vermicelli*	Cauliflower
Pasta	Wheatgerm	Broccoli
White or Brown rice	Dried beans	Eggplant
	Lentils	Mushroom
Rice Cakes	Sweet Potato	Cabbage
Sweets	Yams	Artichokes
Sausage Rolls	Soy beans	Peppers
Potatoes	Chickpeas	Spinach
Turnips	Fresh and dried fruit*	Squash
Parsnips		
Corn		
Beetroot		
Carrots		
Cornflour		
Refined cereals		
– puffed rice		
– corn flakes		
– Special K		
Alcohol		
– Beer	*These are	
– Spirits	exceptions which	
Chocolate	are explained later.	

The Method

When it becomes your desire to lose some weight, then one need only focus on the type of carbohydrates that you are including with your meal. So we use this approach.

First remove all the bad carbohydrates from the scene, do not let a single one touch your lips, just concern yourself with the other two categories of carbohydrates. You can now add to this a third element. The other part of a balanced diet is the proteins and lipids.

So now the protein and lipids are in the third column. As earlier stated, the best source of protein is first class protein, namely that found in meats, dairy food and seafood. As well as this it also contains lipids, which are the oils and fats, so I have included those in this column.

The selection of food that you can choose from is the moderate carbohydrates, good carbohydrates, and proteins and lipids. The bad carbohydrates are out of the picture for good, so the list of foods should look something like this next table.

1 Moderate Carbohydrates	2 Good Carbohydrates	3 Protein and Lipids
Whole Wheat	Alfalfa Sprout	Meats
– Wheat	Celery	Poultry
– Oats	Bamboo Shoots	Lamb
– Barley	Cucumber	Pork
– Millet	Tomato	Ham
– etc	Radish	Beef
Rye Bread*	Lettuce	Veal
Bran	Cauliflower	Rabbit
Basmati Rice*	Broccoli	Kangaroo
Fresh Pasta*	Egg Plant	Eggs
Bean thread	Mushroom	Fish
noodles*	Cabbage	Lobster
Wheat Germ	Artichokes	Crab
Dried Beans	Peppers	Prawns/shrimp
Dried peas	Spinach	Butter
Lentils	Squash	Margarine
Sweet Potato		Cheese
Yam		Oils
Soy Beans		
Chickpeas		
Fresh and dried		
fruit*		

Hey, it's starting to look better already, but before we go any further let's have a look at these exceptions.

The exceptions

Pasta: The reason is that any pasta that takes more than five minutes to cook, is going to have a high GI. This is because the heat from cooking causes the carbohydrates in the pasta to swell and increase their surface area over time, meaning more sugar is absorbed when you eat it. Let me put it another way. Try to imagine at a microscopic level that the carbohydrates in the pasta look like tennis balls before you cook them, and when you heat them they start to expand, so that after say ten minutes they have totally expanded to the size of basketballs. Well the less time it takes to cook, the less they expand. Do you know the old trick of throwing the pasta against the wall to see if it is cooked? It's cooked because it's the expanded sugar that makes it stick to the wall.

Where I come from, fresh pasta is usually fettuccine. You either make it yourself, or buy it at a deli or super-market, and it is one of the few types of pasta that is cooked in less than five minutes, but here's where you need to be careful. **Don't overcook the pasta.** If it is still not cooked after five minutes, it is not the right kind.

Basmati rice: This is the rice that they use in India and the type you get if you go to an Indian resturant. 'Mahatma Premium' is a popular brand in Australia. This rice has carbohydrate polymers that are different to other rice. On a microscopic level, normal rice carbohydrates are chains that are strung together with many branches, which end up giving them a greater surface area. When boiled they produce more glucose.

Basmati rice, on the other hand, has its carbohydrates in a single chain, and this makes it a moderate carbohydrate on the GI. It doesn't produce as much glucose, and that's why normal rice sticks together whilst Basmati rice falls apart after being cooked. Unlike pasta, it isn't the cooking time that matters, it is actual structure of the carbohydrates that makes them different.

Fructose: This is the sugar found in fruit, and is a type of sugar that's quite friendly to the body and doesn't cause the blood sugar level to peak. Fruit doesn't appear to cause the blood sugar level spikes that some carbohydrates produce, with the exception of banana and some melons, which contain a lot of glucose.

Pure rye bread: This is hard to find and feels like a brick, but has a low GI. Fortunately there is another type that is made from triticale that is easily found in the supermarkets. In Australia the brand name is 'Performax' by Country Life Bakeries

The Combinations for Weight Loss.

So you have now got rid of all the bad carbohydrates from your diet, and that's great, but unfortunately it won't be enough to help you lose weight. To ensure that you are going to lose weight you now have to know the art of combining the different elements of the above lists into meals. The combinations produce two types of meals.

The first is an all-carbohydrate meal, which is a combination of the moderate and good carbohydrates. Because the moderate carbohydrates in this type of meal can raise your blood sugar level to the point where insulin may be released, we don't combine fats with this, so I have called it a **carbohydrate only meal**.

The other I call a **protein meal**. It is a combination of only the good carbohydrates that will not raise your blood sugar level, which have been combined with protein from meats and seafood. Because in this second option you are barely raising your blood sugar level, the risk of insulin being released has been removed, and therefore the fats cannot be absorbed. As a result, added fats and oils, as well as those found in meats, can be included. But we will look at this in more detail later. First, let's focus on the carbohydrate only meal .

Carbohydrate Only Meal

With the first meal, you are combining the moderate and good carbohydrates together. Because this meal contains elements that can affect the blood sugar level moderately, then there is a chance of insulin being released. This is nothing to worry about because it is only a small amount, and the excess sugar that would have to be metabolised, would probably never be converted to fat, simply because there just isn't enough. However, we don't want to be eating fats at this time because the possible arrival of insulin may cause those fats to be absorbed. This is what we do not want when trying to lose weight.

As a result, this meal is one which should contain no fat at all. Zero fat should be your goal when eating a combination of these two categories of carbohydrates. If you were going to stir-fry the vegetables, you would use water and a nonstick fry pan instead of oil. So the carbohydrate only meal would be a combination of the lists 1 and 2.

The meals that can be created from these two lists would be suitable for breakfast, lunch, or dinner if need be. But I find that breakfast is almost always a carbohydrate meal for me. It may be some fruit followed by cereal, or 'Performax' bread with a spread of Vegemite.*

*Vegemite (*proper noun*): [veg-e-mite] Black tar-like substance of indefinable quality that Australians have loved for generations. 'Crickey! we've run out of *Vegemite!*'

1 Moderate Carbohydrates	2 Good Carbohydrates	3 Protein and Lipids

Whole Wheat
– Wheat
– Oats
– Barley
– Millet
– etc
Rye Bread*
Bran
Basmati Rice*
Fresh Pasta*
Bean thread
   noodles*
Wheat Germ
Dried Beans
Dried peas
Lentils
Sweet Potato
Yam
Soy Beans
Chickpeas
Fresh and dried
   fruit*
	Alfalfa Sprout
	Celery
	Bamboo Shoots
	Cucumber
	Tomato
	Radish
	Lettuce
	Cauliflower
	Broccoli
	Eggplant
	Mushroom
	Cabbage
		Meats
		Poultry
		Lamb
		Pork
		Ham
		Beef
		Veal
		Rabbit
		Kangaroo
		Eggs
		Fish
		Lobster
		Crab
		Prawns/shrimp
		Butter
		Margarine
		Cheese
		Oils

If you wanted to continue with this type of meal you could create a lunch out of fettuccini with vegetables and Napoli sauce. Dinner might also be a risotto or stir fried vegetables. However, you could also choose to eat a protein meal should it be your desire. I prefer to start with a carbohydrate meal for breakfast, have a protein meal at lunch and either a carbohydrate meal or protein meal in the evening. Once you understand how to use this information you can be flexible. Let's now look at the protein meal.

The Protein Meal

I call this a protein meal, just to make it an easy reference. To be more accurate, you could call it a low glycemic index carbohydrate lipid protein combination. I don't know about you, but 'can I take your order please', 'Yes I'll have a low glycemic index carbohydrate lipid protein combination please' just doesn't work for me, so we're going to just refer to it as a protein meal.

The protein meal is the combination of the last two categories. It's a combination of the good carbohydrates, and the meats and fats of category three. Because the carbohydrates that you're combining have a very low glycemic index, they will not cause a rise in your blood sugar level. Imagine that you tried to get your BSL up by eating a whole bag of mushrooms. Regardless of the amount you are putting in your system, it is also the time it takes to digest that determines the rise in the BSL as well. The body would be unable to extract sufficient amounts of glucose in time to make a big dent in the BSL. If you found a way, however, of extracting the sugar and made a concentrate, then that would be a different story. Because of this, the amount at which the blood sugar level rises is well below the threshold at which insulin is produced, so the risk of absorbing the fats has gone. The fact that you are eating fats and oils is of little consequence, because the body cannot metabolise the fats without insulin present.

The combination of categories 2 and 3 gives you the protein meal.

1 Moderate Carbohydrates	2 Good Carbohydrates	3 Protein and Lipids
Whole Wheat	Alfalfa Sprout	Meats
– Wheat	Celery	Poultry
– Oats	Bamboo Shoots	Lamb
– Barley	Cucumber	Pork
– Millet	Tomato	Ham
– etc	Radish	Beef
Rye Bread*	Lettuce	Veal
Bran	Cauliflower	Rabbit
Basmati Rice*	Broccoli	Kangaroo
Fresh Pasta*	Egg Plant	Eggs
Bean thread	Mushroom	Fish
noodles*	Cabbage	Lobster
Wheat Germ	Artichokes	Crab
Dried Beans	Peppers	Prawns/shrimp
Dried peas	Spinach	Butter
Lentils	Squash	Margarine
Sweet Potato		Cheese
Yam		Oils
Soy Beans		
Chickpeas		
Fresh and dried		
fruit*		

These combinations provide you with a wider variety of more interesting dishes. This is where your knowledge of the GI becomes very attractive.

Unfortunately our bodies seem to have had a long time 'love affair' with fats. Unbeknown to us, this courtship has been played out in the reflection of bad food combinations that we have mysteriously found so appealing. Now you can continue the affair whilst at the same time practising a gastronomic version of 'safe sex'. Being careful not to raise your blood sugar level whilst eating fats allows you to forget about the risk of expanding your waistline or raising cholesterol.

When eating the protein meal, the one thing that you have to watch out for is not allowing <u>any</u> hidden sugars from finding their way into the meal. It may be OK to allow yourself to enjoy this type of meal, but by unwittingly including something that will raise your blood sugar levels, and all that good work will be undone. Salad dressings, for example, can often contain sugar. In this case I find that some olive oil is quite adequate here. Sauces frequently contain sugar or corn flour as a thickener, so when eating out, or buying things off the shelf, you need to be certain that the ingredients are not bad carbohydrates.

This may seem a little daunting at first, but having to separate out these undesirable things can be quite enlightening. When I first started using this way of eating I was amazed to find sugar in almost everything that we eat. Trying to buy something from the supermarket shelf that did not list sugar or flour as an ingredient was almost impossible, although it did reveal how all the hidden sugars find their way into your diet. The next time you go to the supermarket is going to be a very interesting experience. Finding the highly prized commodities that aren't contaminated with sugar or flour can be more difficult than you might expect. With a little lateral thinking and a sprinkling of determination, I was able to come up with a few and you can see these reflected in the recipes in the following chapter.

Carbohydrate/Lipid Combinations

Before you begin the job of eating your way back to being happy and healthy again, there are just a few more things that you should be aware of.

Carbohydrate/lipid combinations are foods that are a combination of sugars and fats that we can't separate into two distinct categories. These carbohydrates are sufficient to raise our BSL and they contain fat. Consequently when it comes to weight loss, they also have to retreat. Here are the main offenders:

milk, soy flour, egg noodle, peanuts, liver, coconut, olives, chestnuts, water chestnuts, oysters and scallops.

'Oh come on now, everybody knows that peanuts are fattening, now you know why.' Olives? No big surprise. Don't worry, it's not the end of the world. When it comes to weight loss you need to be relentless. I promise your desire to eat these things, will pass, because your perception associated with these foods also changes. The longer you follow this way of eating, the more amazed you will become at your indifference to some foods that you used to pound the table for with excitement. On the subject of milk, the first thing people ask is, 'How am I going to get calcium in my diet?' My reply is that the advertisement produced by the dairy industry is obviously working. Milk is not the only form of calcium.

There are richer sources than milk. Sesame seeds for example are the highest, but in this case my suggestion is to drink soy milk. There are calcium-enriched ones available, but because you can still eat cheeses, you can include the richest source of calcium as far as dairy goes which is parmesan cheese! Why cheese but not milk? Because milk is mostly lactose (a sugar) and a little fat, while cheese is mostly fat and a little lactose.

Time Windows

As explained earlier, throughout the day you are free to choose between these two types of meals on a meal-to-meal basis. Personally I find it easiest to have a carbohydrate breakfast followed by a protein lunch. Lunch is my main meal of the day, and I prefer to have a protein meal as the largest meal. Dinner carries less importance. It can be either a carbohydrate or protein one, so I'm less concerned (as long as I don't have to cook!) Although you can swap between these two types of meals, there is a window of time that has to be considered when you swap from one to the other. 'OK thinking caps on...'

Because the **carbohydrate meal** contains elements that affect your blood sugar level, you need to wait at least **three hours** for your blood sugar level to come down if you wish to eat anything with fat in it because it normally takes about three hours for the blood sugar level to return to normal.

The **protein meal**, on the other hand, may contain fats, but the carbohydrate contained in it does not raise the blood sugar level sufficiently to be a problem. However, it is very important to avoid anything that will raise your blood sugar level for at least **five hours** after the meal. When you eat lipids and proteins, the body tries to absorb the fat first. After the food leaves the stomach, it passes through the duodenum and it takes about five hours for it to pass through. This means that you have to wait before having anything that will bring your blood sugar level up. So how does this work in practice?

Let us assume, for example, that you have had a carbohydrate breakfast that contained cereals with a moderate glycemic index. This means that for the next three hours you're going to have a moderately raised blood sugar level. So after breakfast you must avoid eating anything that has fat in it, like a piece of cheese for example. Let's imagine that you then wait until lunch time when you decide to have chicken and salad, a protein meal that contains some fats. After lunch you would need to wait five hours before you had anything that was going to raise your blood sugar level, like a piece of fruit as a snack a few hours later.

It is pretty simple really. Wait three hours after having a carbohydrate meal before eating any fats, and wait five hours after eating fats before raising your blood sugar level. But what about this scenario?

You have the same carbohydrate breakfast, and at mid morning, some two hours later, you have a few more moderate carbohydrates like fruit. As a result you realise that you will have to wait another three hours for your blood sugar level to come down after eating the fruit.

It is almost lunch time. At this point you have a choice. If you wanted to eat a protein meal, you would have to wait three hours from the time you ate the fruit, for your blood sugar level to come down. This would stop the fats contained in the protein meal from being absorbed.

On the other hand, you could have another 'carbo-hydrate only' meal without fats for lunch instead, say like fresh pasta. In my opinion it is probably best to 'roll on' with the carbohydrate lunch an hour or so later, as it better to eat at the same time each day, than to have to wait. If you wanted to eat protein that day I would wait until dinner.

Whilst on the same point, let's consider a different scenario. Imagine that you have had a protein dinner and have been very good by selecting the right carbohydrate/protein combinations for that meal. A couple of hours later you are offered something sweet, let's say a mint or some gum. Although you have done very well by eating correctly to begin with, if later you ate something that raised your blood sugar level, insulin would be released and cause those fats contained in the meal that you ate a few hours before, to be absorbed. 'Oops!'. Because you are still in that five-hour window after eating your protein meal, you still cannot afford to raise your blood sugar level.

> Time windows only apply when swapping from one type of meal to another. Wait three hours after a carb meal before eating a protein meal and wait five hours after a protein meal before eating a carb meal.

Eating from either of these two menus is enormous fun. As you become more familiar with this way of eating, your skill at negotiating food combinations also improves. It will just be automatic. The better you become at applying your understanding, the better your result will be.

Next is an example of how your week's eating requirement may look when you are using this way of eating. I have to admit that I personally eat a simpler fare than this, but it is just to let you know that if you wanted to, you could afford to be extravagant and eat like this all the time.

Just remember this is for weight loss.

DAY	Monday	Tuesday	Wednesday	Thursday	Friday	Saturday	Sunday
Breakfast	Muesli	Poached egg and spinnach	Toast and tomato	Cinnamon and bulger with fruit	Zucchini and cheese omelette	Porridge	Bacon and eggs
Lunch	Risotto and fresh dill	Cauliflower and cream cheese soup	Traditional Caesar Salad	Bacon and cheese omelette	spicy roast vegies and paella	Curried cream of chicken soup	Warm red chicken curry salad
Dinner	Chicken and proscuitto	Greek style fish	Roast lamb and pesto	Seafood chowder	Chicken cacciatore	Roast sweet potato with spicy beans	Beef and leek with lemon dressing

Fairly restrictive starvation diet... Not! The amazing thing is that you can eat like this and actually be losing weight. Think about how much energy you would have to be using just by chewing alone!

I have included these recipes later on in the book, with so much choice you shouldn't have trouble finding something to eat. They have been divided into two categories, namely protein meals and carbohydrate meals, to make it easy to follow.

But Wait There's More...

There are only a few things left to this formula. One of the last elements that can be found in a normal diet that can still raise your blood sugar level is caffeine. It is not unusual to have a cup of tea or coffee after having a meal, but unfortunately the caffeine contained in these beverages will also cause insulin to be released. When it comes to eating the protein meal, you do not want the untimely release of insulin to cause the meal to become fattening for you. So how does one avoid this?

Unfortunately the only solution to having your glycemically correct cake and eating it too, is to drink beverages that do not contain caffeine. There are teas that are free of caffeine, and there has been decaffeinated coffee around for quite some time. As much as I dislike the thought of people drinking decaffeinated coffee because of all the other nasty things that it does to your system, some people absolutely need to have coffee, and then it is the only viable alternative.

Teas on the other hand are not as dramatic. Herbal teas are in abundance. One tea in particular is Madura tea. It is a black small leaf tea that is very similar in taste and appearance to English tea. This particular tea does not contain any caffeine, is low in tannin, and is available at most supermarkets. I am sure that there are others. It is one of my favourites, and as long as you don't add too much soy milk, you should still be able to maintain a low glycemic index and have it with protein meals.

When it comes to soy milk, there is a plethora of products on the market at the moment, but unfortunately it is not possible to give you a list of the best brands to have. The only thing to do is to have a look at the amount of sugar that the product contains. The type that you would be interested in is the kind that has the lowest amount of sugar. Incredibly, soy milk also seems to suffer from the burden of having added sweeteners or malt, so be wary. The brand that we use is called Australia's Own malt free soy milk.

Tea on its own has been shown to reduce the risk of skin cancer. This is great news for Australians and I was very pleased to read that the combination of tea and soy combined together dramatically reduces the risk of prostate cancer. Now that has got to be a good thing because this is the biggest killer amongst men. Switching to tea can be actually make you live longer for a number of reasons. So drink up fellas. Coffee, conversely has no known health benefits other that keeping you awake if you have to stay up for some reason.

Give Us This Day, Our Daily Bread Addiction

From my experience when using this style of eating, bread can be one of those additions that can cause problems. Finding bread that does not have an alarming GI is actually difficult. As I earlier reported, pure rye bread or 'Performax' is the only type of bread that comes close to having a moderate GI. However the darker the rye bread, the better. Eventually you end up eating an almost black rye, like the German pumpernickel bread, just to be on the safe side. 'Performax' is more like brown bread.

It is my personal belief that if you wish to be really successful when it comes to losing weight, then it is best to avoid eating bread entirely. I say this because over the years of helping people with their weight, I have seen that those who tried to include bread with their menu had more difficulty losing weight than those who didn't.

The reason why bread can cause such difficulty is because of the way in which flour is prepared. Last century we did not have the technology to produce exceptionally fine flour, but mills have developed stainless steel rollers that are able to crush the grain with tremendous force. As a result, flour was able to be ground to a very fine consistency. Unfortunately, this technique has managed to grind the grain of the wheat so fine that all the carbohydrates within the grain are now liberated, and very easily absorbed in the digestive tract. Consequently, bread typically has a high GI.

This does not mean that bread has to be totally removed from your diet. It's just that beyond the pure rye and 'Performax' it may be difficult to find a really good bread that has a moderate GI. One of the problems is that bread-makers tend to mix different types of flours together. The packet may say 'rye bread', but when you read the ingredients there can also be soy flour, or bleached flour included, so again you have to read the labels. It is my opinion though, that you will receive better results by not eating bread at all. For myself, I seldom eat bread. Besides making it difficult to balance the blood sugar, I find that the yeast can make you feel bloated. When one looks at white bread for example, it's pure glucose. You would get the same result if you were eating cake. It's no coincidence that often people who come to see me who are suffering with a weight problem, also suffer from bread addiction.

It should be quite easy for someone who is trained well in Chinese medicine to tell if a person eats too much sweet food. Sometimes when I meet an overweight patient who, obviously to me, has a sugar problem, I might ask if they have a sweet tooth. Often the vigorous reply is that they do not. My next question is normally, "Do you like eating bread?" Almost always the eyes widen, the head lolls about and the person almost always replies, "I love my bread..."

It is always a revelation when you explain that one reason that they are overweight is because bread is almost pure glucose. The body has to metabolise it, and the result is that it is fattening.

Quite often a person can be over-weight yet hardly eat anything. The reason is simple. A little high energy food each day will keep you exactly at the same weight and every so often when you binge eat, the extra energy gets stored away so the weight slowly creeps up. I've often use the analogy of a credit card. How often have you received your statement and said 'How did that happen?' The debt just keeps slowly adding until before you know it you're struggling to pay it off. The way one can accumulate weight is very similar and eating high energy food like bread is a good way of staying 'in the red'.

One more point about bread. Every so often a person will find a bread that actually has a moderate GI (you can look some up on the internet). What it doesn't tell you is the amount of fat and oil that is in it as well, so sometimes the bread has a moderate GI but is high in fat. Moderate GI and fat? So sorry, 'Talk to the hand' cos the docs not list'nin...'

CHAPTER 3

Compelling Reasons

Hypoglycemia

You may have already heard about hypoglycemia. Although it may seem to be one of those 'fad' types of problems, it is in fact quite real. Hypoglycemia is a description for when your blood sugar level falls below the normal amount. The type of symptoms that can occur include: fatigue, mental confusion, mild depression and withdrawal, irritability, lack of concentration and digestive disturbances. Having read this far, you may already have some insight into why hypoglycemia has suddenly become such a problem over the past few years. Western medicine still struggles to recognise that hypoglycemia actually exists outside of insulin dependent diabetics.

The funny part is that without the GI, just about every meal you eat can make you hypoglycemic. It's just that with some people, it can have a really big effect.

Before seeing me, some patients have consulted a regular doctor, only to be told to go and eat barley sugars!

Bad carbohydrates, as we know are the kind that raise your blood sugar level past the point where insulin is released. What happens is the pancreas, after years of having to pump out so much insulin to combat the blood sugar level 'spikes' eventually gets a little tired and starts to overcompensate. Instead of releasing the exact amount of insulin needed to lower the blood sugar levels, the pancreas develops a knee jerk reaction to bad carbohydrates. When they cause the blood sugar levels to go sky rocketing up, the pancreas reacts by releasing too much insulin into the bloodstream. What typically occurs is the excess insulin drives the blood sugar levels way down. By metabolising and getting rid of the glucose, a person can go from having too much glucose in the blood, to not enough.

The actual mechanics of it is more like this. What initially happens when you have eaten a bad carbohydrate, is that for the first half-hour the blood sugar level starts to rise. Insulin is then released, and over the next half hour the insulin metabolises the excess blood sugar, and it begins to drive the glucose down to its normal limit. But because the pancreas has overcompensated, there will be an excess of insulin excreted. This excess continues to convert the glucose in the blood, lowering the blood sugar level even further. As a result, you begin to experience hypoglycemia.

This will continue for the next two hours. During this time the first thing that you will notice is tiredness. Have you ever wondered why you experience a kind of 'mussy' head, and find it difficult to concentrate? As well as the above symptoms, there is one overriding quality to this hypoglycemic phase. During the next two hours you will have a craving for more bad carbohydrates.

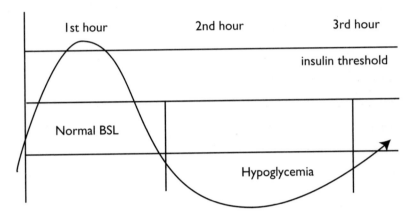

When you think about it, this would be perfectly natural. Your body at this time does not have enough sugar in the bloodstream, and as a result it is telling you that you have to raise the blood sugar level back up again, which the body wants to do as fast as possible. The best way of doing this is by eating something that will produce a lot of glucose.

This is the amazing part, because you will tend to overlook things that have a moderate GI as the body is in a sort of 'crisis situation', and will steer you towards the bad carbohydrates every time. Here we have the basis of sugar craving and sugar addiction. Because you are now craving more sugar, it is very likely that you will eat another bad carbohydrate, and although this will restore the blood sugar level, it will also cause the whole cycle to repeat. A few hours after eating the initial bad carbohydrates, you are once again sending your blood sugar level up. The pancreas responds in the same way again.

The whole process from beginning to end takes about three hours, but you will start getting the signal to increase the blood sugar after about two hours. That is usually why you can crave 'something sweet' and still feel hungry a few hours after a meal.

Studies have shown that the inclusion of bad carbs in a person's diet causes a tendancy to eat 20% more food than normal.

By now you are probably realising that if it is a three hour cycle, it's like a roller coaster going up and down three times a day, every day. If we have to overcompensate with our eating, then inevitably gaining weight is going to be a problem. This is a vicious cycle that I feel is at the heart of a lot of eating problems and one which has also been exploited by some of the fast food manufacturers worldwide.

Why would 'Take-Away' food chain giants use alarming amounts of sugar in their food? One thing for certain is that people will always asscociate that particular version of take away with the need to satisfy their hunger fast whenever they need another sugar fix. Not only will they tend to over eat but once the hunger has gone it won't be long before they will be coming back for more.

Releasing Less Insulin Keeps You Younger

Massachusetts General Hospital in Boston has made a remarkable discovery about a particular gene that can slow the cellular ageing process in human beings. The gene is switched on and off by insulin.

Cells obtain energy by combining glucose with oxygen, a process called metabolic oxidation, which inevitably creates highly reactive atoms called free radicals. Free radicals can damage DNA and disrupt healthy cells. When cells become damaged, the body quickly replaces them. Free radical damage is one of the things that causes premature ageing.

One only needs to look at a smoker to see premature ageing that is a result of free radical damage. The chemical in cigarette smoke produces an enormous number of free radicals. Free radical damage can also lead to diseases like cancer.

Experiments with mice on a low carbohydrate diet have demonstrated that when insulin is not being released, this newly-discovered gene switches on and causes the cells in the body to begin to burn glucose at a highly efficient rate. Because the cells are now operating more efficiently, then there is less oxidation occurring, and as a result, less damaging free radicals are being formed. Not only did the mice have more energy, they also lived longer, up to 40% longer than their litter mates on an unrestricted diet. Many of my patients have also reported a remarkable lift in their energy levels beyond just carrying less weight.

There is a direct correlation to human counterparts. It has been observed that people who live for an extraordinarily long time and survive on a low carbohydrate diet are often thin. They avoid the peaks in their blood sugar level, unlike people on an unrestricted diet.

Credible evidence from research on native peoples, like the herdsmen of Pakistan's Hunza valley, and the Indians of Mexico's Sierra Madre mountains who live on simple and Spartan diets shows that they do live longer and that a few can reach an incredible age.

More recent research has also shown that if mice are allowed to eat between 20–30% less food, then their life expectancy extends dramatically. People on a long-term low-carbohydrate diet eat about 20% less than average. Scientists have concluded that the life expectancy on such a diet could go as high as 130 years. Only time will tell.

Obesity and the West's Consumption of Sugar

Recently the WHO announced that people in the Western World are becoming more obese. In fact, 50% more obese people now make up the population on average. Their advice to a waiting world was that 'People need to cut down on fat in their diet!' I had to laugh. Some of the populations that were mentioned actually eat less fat than ever before, yet they are still suffering from the same problem. You may recall that earlier I cited a study that found that Westerners are eating almost 40 times more sugar than they did at the beginning of the 1800s, as if it could not be more glaringly obvious to you what the problem might be. In a study here in Australia, *Choice* magazine put together a survey of the top ten items in peoples shopping trolly. What do you expect they found? Milk, bread, vegies? *Choice* reported that the top 4 items were in fact cola drinks!

Diabetes

As I earlier explained, the Glycemic Index was first developed by the Diabetics Association of America in the late '70s and early '80s. Up until then they had been taking the advice of the nutritionists who believed that complex carbohydrates were what diabetics needed to eat. Unsurprisingly, diabetics were having a difficult time in controlling their blood sugar level. Naturally if you are going to control your blood sugar level in such a way that very little insulin is released, then of course it will have a beneficial effect on the pancreas.

I remember the time when one of my patients asked me whether I thought that this information would be helpful for controlling his mother's blood sugar level. His mother was a type 1 diabetic who required insulin injections. She had recently been to see a naturopath who had advised her to drink a large glass of carrot juice every morning. Strangely enough her blood sugar level skyrocketed every time. Since following my advice, she and other patients like her have been able to reduce the amount of insulin that they require on a daily basis. Some have actually reported to me that they have not needed to take their insulin for months at a time.

As far as dealing with diabetes is concerned, this is highly desirable, as there are side effects from having blood sugar reach high levels continuously. By being able to decrease the fluctuations in the blood sugar level, less insulin is required, which flows on to minimise the side effects. An ounce of prevention is worth a pound of cure, so the old saying goes. Reducing the amount of insulin that the pancreas has to pump out over a lifetime will greatly contribute to preventing the risk of mature onset diabetes in a lot of people, don't you think?

Cholesterol and High Insulin Levels

It has also been noted that the persistent presence of a high insulin level in the blood also increases the level of cholesterol and triglycerides. These two factors have been held mostly responsible for blocked arteries and heart disease leading to such emergencies as heart attacks.

Over the years I have recommended that patients suffering from high cholesterol levels follow my advice, and avoid bad carbohydrates to keep their insulin level under control. In every case upon re-examination by their regular doctor, they have reported a fall in their cholesterol level. One doctor even described it as 'a miracle.' Cholesterol is one of those things that in Western medicine still carries a question mark even though cholesterol lowering drugs are prescribed more than any other drug. Western medicine is still undecided about the cholesterol that occurs in the body. One of the problems is that the body actually produces some of the cholesterol itself, so sometimes reducing the amount of cholesterol in a person's diet can still have no effect upon their cholesterol level. Cholesterol may not be the universal evil that it first appeared to be, because it plays a vital role in a number of functions of the body. It is just that you can use the cholesterol level in a person's blood as a rough indication of the risk of heart disease. One of the functions of cholesterol in the body is to line the inner walls of the arteries to make them more elastic, but if there is too much cholesterol, then the arteries begin to bulge in places. The red blood cells go speeding past these bulges, striking and bruising them. Eventually the body sends platelets to the site where the red blood cells have been battering the wall of the artery, and adds them to strengthen the 'speed hump' created by the cholesterol. The platelets are like little tiles that get placed in layers over the bump to shield it.

However, the body can keep adding more platelets if the bulge doesn't go away, and the problem is that the platelets can eventually break loose in one big piece, and go sailing off down the artery. This is known as a blood clot, and the clot can eventually get stuck. If the clot lodges in one of the arteries of the heart, you will have a coronary and this is often fatal. If it lodges in the brain then you will have a stroke, and frequently become paralysed down one side of the body. In either case it is obviously better to avoid the problem altogether. Controlling the blood sugar level has the flow-on effect of reducing the amount of cholesterol that the body produces.

While on the subject of heart disease, it has been widely regarded by the Chinese that the number one cause of heart disease is actually stress. I agree with this view, so if you wish to avoid the risk of heart disease learn how to relax, smell the roses and enjoy life.

Anaerobic Bacteria and Sugar

In the digestive tract there is a combination of bacteria that is referred to as the body's normal intestinal flora. The body needs this to aid in the digestion of food. These bacteria fall into two types: one that prefers oxygen and the other that prefers sugar. Both aerobic and anaerobic bacteria use oxygen to burn sugar, but because the anaerobic bacteria doesn't use very much oxygen, it requires about four times more sugar to survive. Anaerobic bacteria, although a necessary part of the intestinal flora, are not required in great abundance. The aerobic bacteria are however, and they keep the presence of the anaerobic bacteria in check by being in greater numbers.

When there is too much sugar passing through the digestive tract, then the anaerobic bacteria have a very good opportunity to thrive. The presence of an overabundance of anaerobic bacteria causes digestive disturbances. Instead of aiding in the breakdown of foods like aerobic bacteria do, anaerobic bacteria tend to cause more of a fermentation to occur.

You will probably notice that when you eat sugars and bad carbohydrates that it is very common to experience bloating afterwards. This is normally the result of the anaerobic bacteria fermenting because of the presence of the excess sugar. Conversely, bloating is a sure sign that you have eaten the wrong kinds of carbs.

Further complications can ensue if this situation is left unchecked. The bloating causes the abdomen to distend and stretch the surrounding adipose tissue, making it more accessible for fat to accumulate. This is why people develop a beer gut for example. The combination of the sugars, in the form of maltose and yeast causes both distension and weight gain simultaneously.

Yeast is something that also thrives on sugar. Back in the '80s you may have had the experience of seeing a naturopath and being told that you suffered from Candida. It is a type of yeast that can cause an enormous number of problems when it gets out of hand. Unfortunately the list of ailments was quite extensive. It was blamed for anything from bad breath to psychosis.

The funny thing about this is that candida occurs naturally in the body so it is always possible to find its presence. That didn't seem to matter very much because naturopaths everywhere were making a fortune from telling people that they had it. Nowadays, the big candida scare has come and gone and telling everybody that they are suffering from candida is a thing of the past. Please don't misunderstand me, candida is a genuine problem, but it is still a symptom rather than the cause. 'Why does this person have this particular problem?' is the foundation of diagnosis for Chinese Medicine, and discovering the cause provides the answer.

Besides avoiding yeast, the problems of candida are best avoided by not filling yourself with sugar. When a person presents with these types of symptoms, the first thing that I do is remove all the bad carbohydrates from their diet. Often, patients have come to me with severe digestive problems that specialists could not help, only to have a complete reversal of their symptoms. I have always taken this approach first, because if we know that it's not the sugar causing the symptoms, then we can start narrowing down the field of other possibilities. The Chinese approach is to look at the obvious first and if that's not it *then* start eliminating. Western Medicine, conversely, starts at the opposite end by eliminating everything and then reintroducing things one by one.

Another way that the intestinal flora can become out of balance is for a person to take a course of antibiotics. The antibiotics kill off both types of bacteria and once the course has finished the body has to re-establish the bacterial community to function properly. Of course, if there is a lot of bad carbohydrate passing through the digestive tract, then the anaerobic bacteria and yeast get a head start and can dominate. This is why digestive problems like diarrhoea commonly ensue after taking antibiotics, and why it is recommended that you have acidophilus once the course of antibiotics has finished. Acidophilus can reflorinate the gut with the good bacteria and circumvent any problems. You can find it in yoghurt, but there are also tablets and drinks that are specifically designed to deliver the bacteria to the intestines, and it should only be a one-off treatment. Whichever one you choose, just be sure that it doesn't contain sugar. Believe it or not, some manufacturers have fallen into the same practice of adding sugar to sweeten the taste so that people will like it, even though sugar is the basis of the problem.

Stay the same weight forever

After I had become very familiar with this way of weight control, I successfully lost, for me, a considerable amount of weight. It soon became apparent that the problem of putting on weight as I grew older had also evaporated. If you haven't realised already, this knowledge is one of the fundamental reasons why you gain, lose or maintain your weight and therefore the ability to control your weight is now within your control.

I have been using this knowledge now for several years and I am always pleased at how efficiently I have been able to control my weight. Prior to this I was resigned to the fact that as I grew older I was going to gradually put on weight and end up like my dad who had always been a bit on the heavy side and, unfortunately, died at age 64. Don't worry, I was only 12 and too young to have helped him. If only I had known then what I know now. It seemed an inevitable consequence that as the testosterone fell, so too did the metabolism. You may have already had the experience of watching with sadness the youthful waistline gradually giving way. Neither I nor my friends were exceptions. After spending most of my life practising Martial Arts, an unfortunate traffic accident in '94 put that on hold for a few years and I watched, with much disappointment, as these gradual changes to my body started to accelerate. Thank goodness the GI came along, because all I can say now is that I am still the same weight as I was in my twenties and I'll stay that way. As for my friends? Well in their own words 'Fat guys need lovin' too you know'.

Polycystic Ovarian Syndrome (PCOS)

I was quite pleased to read that in the US, doctors have now agreed that a low carb diet is essential for treating PCOS. I had been putting woman on a low carb diet for several years already. Basically, the overabundance of insulin in the blood, as a result of a high carb diet, produces small cysts around the ovaries, which in turn leads to infertility. Each month another egg is produced but instead of going down the fallopian tube it stays around the ovary and becomes a small cyst, like a pimple. Each month there is another, so eventually there are many cysts. Why doesn't the egg go down the fallopian tube? The mucus is too heavy for one thing and doesn't allow it. Why? Too much sugar in the diet.

Over the years I have helped many woman with PCOS. They normally come to me when they find they are having trouble conceiving. We can often get good results after a few months, although sometimes it can be only a matter of weeks. The big joke around the clinic is that I have made lots of women pregnant over the years. But why has PCOS become an epidemic in women's health? Low fat diets are one reason. Low fat means high carbs and, conversely, the rise of fast and processed foods. The resultant increase in weight means an increase in PCOS. When a lady comes to see me who can't conceive and is carrying extra weight around the hips, I usually suggest that she have an ultrasound. More often than not, the results come back that she has PCOS.

Binge Eating

Binge eating is the compulsion to eat too much food. The body actually has mechanisms to tell you to stop eating but we learn to override these when we are young. Having to finish everything on the plate before leaving the table is a good example of this.

When the person focuses completely on eating and ends up eating too much, sometimes they may not eat again until they are starving and so they binge again. This can cause enormous problems for the digestion as well as the person's sense of self esteem. Binge eating can often be compensatory behaviour for other things, however it can also have something to do with the amount of insulin being produced.

When we eat something that gives us a big rise in blood sugar levels, the excess insulin actually binds to receptors in the brain to produce sugar cravings and this can be the signal for us to overeat. Another thing the body does is to reward us for eating high energy food. That's why we go 'mmm yummy', when we eat things that maybe we shouldn't. It's not really that it's yummy, it's because our brain is releasing chemicals to make us want to eat it, just in case we were having second thoughts. You see, our body wants the food more than we do and it will override us if it can. The good news is that when we stop presenting the high energy food to it, it stops and as a result people lose their food cravings. After a little while you will wonder why you ever ate the things you did. What I find ironic is that in spite of our ignorance, our bodies have known about GI for a very long time. When you look at the types of food that most people prefer, it is no coincidence that it's almost always a combination of bad carbs and fats. For many years we have struggled to reduce the amount of fat in our diets, and yet the population has continued to become overweight.

By controlling the chemicals in your brain, your body can guide you to those types of combinations that will best allow you to put on weight. Just look at 'Fast food'. I guar-antee you that in every case, it's a combination of fat and bad carb's. The phenomena behind the growth of these types of outlets is not only because of aggressive and clever marketing, but also the body's love of absorbing energy.

People are easily caught in the trap of lack of exercise and a high energy diet. As the weight increases, the person becomes more sedentary and the need to compensate with high sugar/fat foods goes up. As the years go by, the person eventually reaches a point where everything begins to slow down, energy levels become low and the person now only eats small amounts, but never loses weight.

We have found in these cases that after following *Low Carb Made Easy*, the patients are capable of dropping dramatic amounts of weight in a very short time. 8–10 kg in a couple of weeks is not unusual. It seems the change in momentum catches the body by surprise and it readily gives up the weight.

CHAPTER 4

On Getting Good Results

Combating Sugar Craving With Fruit

Something that you will discover is that whenever you eat a bad carbohydrate you almost immediately begin to crave more bad carbohydrates. The reason behind this is because your body is trying to tell you that you have stumbled on a high energy food source and you should be trying to gorge yourself because it may be in limited supply.

Chemicals in your brain compelling you to continue to eat can have a snowballing effect. As I pointed out earlier, bad carbohydrates lead to food cravings and overeating. We have noticed that this period lasts for approximately three days after breaking the rules. That means that for the next three days you may expect to struggle a little with your renewed sugar cravings, just like any addiction when reintroduced. Fortunately I have found a technique that can shorten this period, should you find that you have somehow inadvertently eaten the wrong things, and heaven knows, now you have this knowledge it would have to be a mistake!

Like I was saying, if you discover that you have somehow 'made a boo boo', then a way of short-cutting the sugar cravings is to have one meal that is only fruit. Fructose is a type of sugar that is very kind to your body and doesn't have such a dramatic effect on your BSL. I have found that it is a type of middle ground when it comes to dealing with sugar addiction. It seems to satisfy your body's desire for sugar, and yet it does not cause an elevated blood sugar level that will lead to further cravings.

I find that if it is possible to simply eat one meal that is entirely fruit, then I seem to be OK by the next meal. The danger associated with eating bad carbohydrates is that you are most likely to continue to eat them once you have started. It is very important to stop this cycle from continuing. By using fruit in this way you can return as quickly as possible to your intended eating patterns.

Why sometimes more is better

One pleasing aspect about using this way of eating is that it makes it very easy to lose weight whilst still being able to eat a fairly normal diet. As with most diets, one has to restrict the intake to lose weight. However, when controlling your BSL, the amount of food that you eat is not an issue. In fact from my experience with helping people lose weight, I notice that sometimes a person has made the mistake of believing that it is necessary to eat less to achieve a results. Occasionally it is because the person is not eating enough food, that he/she is not getting the desired results. The reason why eating more during this period will help you lose weight, is that the extra amount of food you are eating will cause your metabolic rate to increase, because your body needs to work harder to digest the larger amounts of food that you are putting into your system. Having an increased metabolic rate is one of those things that helps with weight loss. Often when people try to lose weight by dieting, they are required to restrict the amount of food they eat. When people start to eat less, the body automatically compensates by slowing the metabolic rate down so you do not burn up as much fuel.

Our body has very sophisticated survival mechanisms. A part of this is its ability to survive in times of famine. Slowing down the metabolic rate is one of these features, as a consequence a slower metabolic rate stops you from burning up your energy reserves. However, when people attempt to lose weight by restricting the amount of food that they eat, they immediately make it more difficult for themselves. One of the very clever things that this style of eating affords, is that you can actually increase your metabolic rate by eating more instead of less.

An interesting point is that it was often believed that overweight people had slow metabolisms, but again this theory had never been tested until recently. It was discovered that overweight people actually had faster metabolisms than people who were of normal weight. The reason behind this is seen to be associated with the extra amount of exertion required to carry the excess weight. Every part of the body is put under strain and it would seem that this increase in effort raises the metabolic rate.

Sometimes a patient tells me that they are overweight because they have a slow metabolism, and I am happy to explain this to them.

The rules can't be broken

What I have found from working with this knowledge is that the guidelines are very clear and that even the smallest 'corner cutting' can bring everything to a halt.

For example, when you are losing weight and you seem to be going well, you get up on to the scales each morning and often see a measurable improvement. On average most people lose about one kilo per week. It seems that even one meal that falls outside of these guidelines, causes your progress to be immediately halted. After a while it is easy to become blasé and fall into the trap of thinking that a slight variation will incur little penalty. You will be amazed when you discover that the retribution is swift and obvious. Make no mistake; this is very sophisticated knowledge. Because you are really out on the cutting edge, then there is little margin for error. So my advice to you is, 'Do not to attempt to bend the rules in any way'. Wait until you have reached a desirable weight, and then you can begin to experiment with these combinations. I have included a section on what to do once you have lost the excess weight. To avoid any confusion, I feel that it is best not to read this section until then. One must be familiar with this technique of weight loss before moving on to the technique of maintaining your weight.

Three things you must do:

1. **Throw out all the bad carbs.** That way there is no temptation for you at home. If you can't throw them out then give them to friends and loved ones.

2. **Prepare food in advance.** This is absolutely critical to success. Pick a day to do some cooking. Choose three or so dishes from the recipes and make a big batch. Have some and than put the rest in the fridge. Take something to heat up for lunch and when you get home from work, there is something to be eaten. I can't stress this point enough. Momentum and continuity needs to be maintained for best results.

3. **Eat more protein meals in the first few weeks.**
By eating more protein meals to begin with you catch the liver by surprise and the weight loss can be quite dramatic in these first few weeks. It's also a good technique if things start to slow down.

These three things are what I always tell someone when first starting out. I know that if you do this then you are sure to get good results.

PART 2

The Food

CHAPTER 5

The 7 Day Meal Planner

This seven-day meal planner aims to give you a good guide to organizing your meals. It will show you how protein and carbohydrate meals can be eaten throughout the day whilst observing the all important time windows.

Looking at the meal planner, you can see that your meals will be a veritable feast; you definitely won't go hungry. In fact, you should remember that you can eat as much food (within reason) as you like. Restricting serving size will actually have a negative effect on your ambitions to improve your health and lose weight.

All the recipes for the meal planner can be found in chapter six, the recipe section of this book. By using the recipe index at the back of the book you can easily find the exact recipe you are looking for.

Remember that the meal planner is only meant as a guide. You can design your own plan that suits your tastes and your time schedule.

DAY 1

Breakfast

1 bowl of muesli with soy milk
1 glass of orange juice
1 cup of tea

Morning tea

1 apple
1 glass of water

Lunch

Risotto with fresh dill and roasted tomato wedges
1 glass of orange juice
1 cup of tea

3 hour interval before dinner

Afternoon tea

Celery, tomato and cucumber slices
1 glass of water

Dinner

Chicken and proscuitto with creamy cheese sauce
Mixed lettuce with light vinaigrette
1 glass of water
1 cup of tea

Supper

4 slices of tasty cheese
1 glass of water

DAY 2

Breakfast

Poached eggs on spinach with garlic dressing

1 cup of decaffeinated coffee

1 glass of water

Morning tea

4 proscuitto roll-ups with brie

1 glass of water

Lunch

Cauliflower and cream cheese soup

1 glass of water

1 cup of tea

Afternoon tea

Sliced celery, tomato and cucumber

1 glass of water

Dinner

Greek style fish

1 glass of water

1 cup of tea

Supper

1 orange

1 glass of water

DAY 3

Breakfast

2 pieces of toast with tomato

1 cup of tea

1 glass of apple juice

3 hour interval before lunch

Morning tea

Celery, tomato and cucumber slices

1 glass of water

Lunch

Traditional Caesar salad

1 cup of tea

1 glass of water

Afternoon tea

.4 slices of ham

1 glass of water

Dinner

Roast lamb and vegetables with cheese sauce and pesto

1 cup of tea

1 glass of water

Supper

4 slices of cheese

1 glass of water

DAY 4

Breakfast

1 bowl of cinnamon bulgur with fresh fruit

1 cup of decaffeinated coffee

1 glass of orange juice

3 hour interval before lunch

Morning tea

Celery, tomato and cucumber slices

1 glass of water

Lunch

Easy bacon and cheese omelette

Mixed lettuce with light vinaigrette

1 cup of tea

1 glass of water

Afternoon tea

4 slices of roast turkey breast

1 glass of water

Dinner

Seafood chowder

1 cup of tea

1 glass of water

Supper

4 slices of cheese

1 glass of water

DAY 5

Breakfast

Zucchini and cheese omelettes with mushrooms in sauce

1 cup of tea

1 glass of water

5 hour interval before lunch

Morning tea

Celery, tomato and cucumber slices

1 glass of water

Lunch

Spicy roasted vegetable paella with chickpeas

1 cup of tea

1 glass of water

3 hour interval before dinner

Afternoon tea

Celery, tomato and cucumber

1 glass of water

Dinner

Chicken cacciatore

Mixed lettuce with light vinaigrette

1 cup of tea

1 glass of water

Supper

Prosciutto roll-ups with brie

1 glass of water

DAY 6

Breakfast

Porridge

1 glass of apple juice

1 cup of tea

3 hour interval before lunch

Morning tea

Celery, tomato and cucumber

1 glass of water

Lunch

Curried cream of chicken soup

1 cup of tea

1 glass of water

5 hour interval before dinner

Afternoon tea

Celery, cucumber and tomato

1 glass of water

Dinner

Roasted sweet potato with spicy bean and tomato sauce

1 cup of tea

1 glass of water

Supper

1 orange

1 glass of water

DAY 7

Breakfast

Roasted tomatoes with haloumi and proscuitto served with garlic mushrooms and crispy bacon

1 cup of tea

1 glass of water

Morning tea

4 slices of turkey breast

1 glass of water

Lunch

Warm red curry chicken salad with salsa verde

1 cup of tea

1 glass of water

Afternoon tea

Prosciutto roll-ups with brie

1 glass of water

Dinner

Kangaroo with leeks and lemon dressing

1 cup of tea

1 glass of water

Supper

4 slices of cheese

1 glass of water

CHAPTER 6

The Recipes

Beverages, Fruit, Bread

Breakfast

Stocks, Dressings, Sauces and Dips

Snacks

Soups

Salads

Side-Dishes

Risottos and Pilaus

Poultry

Meat

Seafood

Eggs and Cheese

Vegetables and Legumes

This is your opportunity to experiment with food combinations. Let imagination be your guide. You can choose a variety of combinations according to your appetite. Remember, the key is to avoid raising your BSL. We have included over 130 recipes that will keep your BSL stable, make you feel both energised and satisfied, and help you lose weight. Browsing over the options, you will notice how accessible and enjoyable preparing your own healthy food can be. We have deliberately tried to make the meals as quick and easy as possible. In fact, I'm sure you will wonder why you didn't eat like this before.

All the meals are very nutritious. However, I do recommend that you take a daily vitamin and mineral supplement as much of the food bought in the supermarket can be nutritionally deficient.

The ingredients used in the recipes should be found relatively easily at your local supermarket. You might find your local delicatessen and Chinese supermarket to be of help if your supermarket sells a limited range of produce.

The recipes are intended to give you an example of the variety of food you can eat. The meals can be altered slightly to suit your tastes but you must still adhere to the carbohydrate guidelines and time windows. Of course when you become more familiar with this method of food combination, you can develop your own recipe ideas.

BEVERAGES, FRUIT, BREAD

Beverages

Fruit

Fruit Salad

Cinnamon Bulgur with Fresh Fruit

Bread

Beverages

Juice: *Carbohydrate*

Being carbohydrate in nature, juice should only be consumed with carbohydrate style meals, never with protein meals. Only drink juice clearly labelled as having no added sugar, or make your own. Apple juice, orange juice and grapefruit juice are all acceptable.

Tea: *Carbohydrate/Protein*

Only use tea that is caffeine free. We use a brand called 'Madura' which is 97% caffeine free. This is acceptable. Please note that green tea, like most black tea, does have caffeine. You may have milk in your tea as it is only a small amount. Do not add sugar.

Herbal Tea: *Carbohydrate/Protein*

Most herbal teas are caffeine free and therefore suitable to have with any meal. Some suggested herbal teas include peppermint and chamomile.

Coffee: *Carbohydrate/Protein*

Use decaffeinated coffee only. You may use a little milk, but do not add any sugar.

Milk: *Carbohydrate/Lipid*

No milk is allowed because it is a combination of sugar and fat together and therefore will be guaranteed to make you fat. If you are concerned about your calcium intake then I suggest eating more cheese or taking a calcium supplement.

Soy Milk: *Carbohydrate*

Soy milk is an excellent alternative to regular milk. Made from soy beans it is classified as a moderate carbohydrate. Choose sugar free soy milk that does not contain maltodextrine. Do not drink too much soy milk. Some on your muesli in the morning and in your cups of tea is permissible.

Beverages you should forget even exist: cola drinks, all soft drinks, all milk drinks, rice milk, cordial, sports drinks, flavoured yoghurt drinks, beer, spirits, regular coffee, energy drinks.

Beverages you should become reaquainted with:

- WATER
- WATER
- WATER

Water is the most thirst-quenching substance known to man. You should have at least 6–8 glass of water per day. You can drink water with any meal and at any time of the day.

Fruit

All fruit is carbohydrate in nature and therefore should not be eaten with protein meals. Remember to observe the time intervals between eating a carbohydrate meal and a protein meal, when eating fruit. It is best to eat fruit on an empty stomach, such as in the morning for breakfast.

Fruits that you can eat include: apples, dried apples, oranges, grapefruit, apricots, dried apricots, cherries, peaches, pears, plums, prunes and strawberries.

Fruits that you should avoid: bananas, kiwi fruit, mango, paw paw, pineapple, rock melon, watermelon, raisins, sultanas, currants, grapes, figs and dates.

Fruit Salad
Carbohydrate

This fruit salad includes a wide range of fruit. Of course you can choose your favourite fruit from the list of acceptable fruit on the previous page. Make sure that the fruit is also in season.

1 pink grapefruit

1 lime

2 oranges

2 pears, peeled, cored and diced

4 apricots, peeled and diced

2 apples, peeled, cored and diced

juice of one orange

4 whole cloves

1 teaspoon cinnamon

Peel and segment grapefruit, lime and oranges. Cut membranes away from segments; discard membranes. Place segments into a large bowl and add all other ingredients. Mix well. Place fruit salad into a covered container and refrigerate 12 hours before serving.

Total cooking time: 20 minutes preparation,12 hours refrigeration
Serves: 4

Cinnamon Bulgur with Fresh Fruit
Carbohydrate

This is great for breakfast or for a snack between carbohydrate meals.

1 cup coarse bulgur (cracked wheat)
2 cups apple juice
1 teaspoon ground cinnamon
½ cup cherries, seeded and halved
2 plums, seeded and chopped
1 apple, peeled, cored and chopped
1 orange, peeled and chopped
Orange zest and sugar free blackberry jam to garnish

Mix bulgur, apple juice and cinnamon well. Place in a sealed container and leave to soak overnight in the refrigerator. Combine softened bulgur with fruit and mix well. Divide amongst four bowls and garnish with jam and orange zest.

Total cooking time: 12 hours soaking, 20 minutes preparation
Serves: 4

Bread

The subject of bread can be a little tricky because bread is usually made from refined flours and hence has a high glycemic index.

There is only one type of bread that I know of (in Australia) that has a moderately low glycemic index; PerforMax, produced by Country Life Bakeries, is available in most leading supermarkets. PerforMax bread has a glycemic index of 38 and therefore is acceptable for use with carbohydrate style meals. In other countries you will be looking for triticale bread. Check the packaging for labelling indicating the glycemic index; you will be looking for a glycemic index of less than 50 for the 'glucose' glycemic index scale.

Bread made solely with rye flour should also have a moderate glycemic index. However most rye breads have other flours added to them like soya flour (which is a sugar and fat combination) and potato (which is definitely not part of your health plan). So, unless you are absolutely sure that the bread is 'pure' rye bread, I would avoid rye based breads.

If you have found a bread that claims to have a low glycemic index or to be 'pure' rye bread then I would assess for any of the following:

- Do I crave this particular food?
- Do I feel like eating the whole loaf in one sitting?
- Do I feel bloated after eating this bread?
- Do I feel hungry again 30 minutes to 2 hours after eating this bread?
- When eating it I don't seem to be losing any weight or I can't seem to lose any more weight.

If you have answered 'yes' to any of the above questions then chances are that the bread you are eating has a high glycemic index and is very unhealthy for you. You can apply this same philosophy to other carbohydrates whose glycemic index or sugar content you are unsure of.

If you are really having a hard time achieving your health goals then I would suggest eliminating bread altogether.

BREAKFAST

Toast

Muesli

Roma Tomatoes and Haloumi with Mushrooms and Bacon

Zucchini and Cheese Omelettes

Porridge

Poached Eggs on Spinach with Garlic Dressing

Toast
Carbohydrate

Make sure you have thoroughly read and understood the section on bread before making your toast.

You cannot have any protein/lipid type foods with your toast. This includes butter, cream, cheese and meats.

The following is a list of some good toast serving ideas:

- Toast spread with jam. Ensure that the jam is sugar-free. Some suggested brands are *St Dalfour*'s and *Smucker's Simply 100% Spreadable Fruit.*

- Toast spread with Vegemite or equivalent substitute.

- Toast topped with fresh tomato and herbs. I usually dice the tomato and briefly stir-fry it in a non-stick pan, before adding some fresh herbs of choice, cracked black pepper and salt. For variety add sautéed onion and/or mushroom.

Muesli
Carbohydrate

I have been unable to find any breakfast cereal that has a moderate or low GI (the exception is Kelloggs All Bran which you can use in this recipe). At the request of clients I have purchased different cereals and sampled them for their carbohydrate effect. I have found all to be unsatisfactory. The moral of the story is, don't purchase breakfast cereals, instead have this fresh and wholesome home-made museli at your breakfast table.

4 cups rolled oats (not quick oats)
¾ cup fresh apple juice
1 teaspoon cinnamon
1½ cups processed bran (no added sugar)
½ cup unprocessed bran
1 cup dried apple slices, chopped
1 cup dried apricots, chopped

Combine oats, apple juice and cinnamon in a large baking dish, mix through well. Place in oven at 200°C for 20-30 minutes until golden brown. Stir occasionally. Combine roasted oats, processed and unprocessed bran, dried apples and dried apricots. Serve with malt free soy milk or sugar free juice. Store in a well sealed container. Keeps for up to 2 weeks.

Total cooking time: 20 minutes cooking,10 minutes preparation
Serves: 8 bowls

Roma Tomatoes with Haloumi and Prosciutto served with Garlic Mushrooms and Crispy Bacon

Protein

A Greek style cooked breakfast, easy to prepare and delicious to eat.

2 tablespoons olive oil

4 Roma tomatoes, halved lengthways

1 tablespoon mixed dried herbs

Salt and pepper to taste

125g haloumi cheese, sliced 1cm thick

8 thin slices of prosciutto

250g button mushrooms, peeled, stalks removed

2 tablespoons olive oil, extra

2 cloves garlic, chopped finely

1 tablespoon mixed dried herbs, extra

1 medium tomato, diced

2 tablespoons lemon juice

8 rashers rindless bacon

Extra fresh parsley to garnish

Coat Roma tomatoes in olive oil and sprinkle with dried herbs and seasoning. Place under a hot grill for 10 minutes.

Place haloumi under a hot grill for 3–5 minutes each side until golden brown. Place haloumi slices on top of tomato halves, wrap with a slice of prosciutto, return to the grill for a further 3 minutes.

Place bacon under a hot grill, turning once until browned and crispy.

Heat extra olive oil in a saucepan, add mushrooms and garlic and stir-fry 3 minutes until mushrooms are soft. Add extra dried herbs, tomato, lemon juice and seasoning. Stir-fry an additional 3 minutes.

Divide Roma tomatoes with haloumi and prosciutto between four plates, do the same with the garlic, mushrooms and bacon. Garnish with fresh parsley.

Total cooking time: 20 minutes
Serves: 4

Zucchini and Cheese Omelettes with Mushrooms in a Creamy Sauce

Protein

4 eggs

4 tablespoons cream

Dash salt and pepper

1 small zucchini, grated and squeezed of excess fluid

½ cup grated tasty cheese

2 tablespoons butter

250g button mushrooms

½ lemon juice

2 tablespoons fresh parsley, finely chopped

2 tablespoons marscapone cheese

Extra parsley to garnish

Break eggs into a large mixing bowl and beat well. Add cream, seasoning, zucchini and cheese and mix well. Heat a medium oiled frypan, add half the omelette mixture. Fork mixture until lightly set then fold omelette in half. Continue to cook over medium heat a further 2 minutes. Remove omelette, keep warm whilst cooking other half of egg mixture using the same process. Meanwhile, melt butter in a saucepan and add mushrooms. Cook 5 minutes or until mushrooms are soft and well cooked. Add juice, parsley and marscapone. Mix well, heating for 1 minute. Serve omelettes onto two pre-heated plates. Spoon over mushrooms. Serve.

Total cooking time: 25 minutes
Serves: 2

Porridge
Carbohydrate

Once again use rolled oats and orange juice with no added sugar for this recipe.

2 cups of rolled oats
1½ cups of soy milk
1 teaspoon of cinnamon
½ teaspoon of nutmeg
½ cup chopped dried apricots
juice of 1 orange

Heat soy milk in a saucepan. Do not boil. Add rolled oats, cinnamon and nutmeg. Bring to the boil, then simmer for 3 minutes. Stir through orange juice and dried apricots.

Total cooking time: 5 minutes
Serves: 2

Poached Eggs on Spinach with Garlic Dressing

Protein

8 eggs

3 tablespoons plain white vinegar

1 teaspoons salt

1 tablespoon dried mixed herbs

315g baby English spinach leaves, washed

1 tablespoon butter

Salt and pepper to taste

½ cup sour cream

1 clove garlic, crushed

1 tablespoon fresh chives, snipped

Extra fresh chives to garnish

Half fill a large saucepan with water. Bring to the boil then reduce heat to a low simmer. Add salt and vinegar. Individually break the eggs into a bowl then slide into the simmering water. Cook eggs 2-3 minutes until they set.

Steam spinach until just beginning to wilt. Drain and stir through butter and seasoning. Combine sour cream, garlic and chives. Arrange spinach onto 4 plates, top with two eggs each and serve over garlic dressing. Garnish with extra fresh chives.

Total cooking time: 10 minutes
Serves: 4

STOCKS, DRESSINGS SAUCES AND DIPS

Vegetable Stock

Chicken Stock

Fish Stock

Red Curry Paste

Green Curry Paste

Masaman Curry Paste

Salsa

Pesto

Creamy Lemon Mayonnaise

Hollandaise Sauce

Light Vinaigrette with Fresh Parsley and Roasted Garlic

Chilli Sauce

Raita

Baba Ghanoush

Hummus

Salmon Dip

Bacon and Onion Dip

Vegetable Stock
Carbohydrate/Protein

2 white onions and skins, finely chopped

8 whole spring onions, finely chopped

1 cup parsley and stalks, chopped

4 stems of rosemary

3 sticks celery and leaves, chopped

3 bay leaves

10 black peppercorns

½ small red chilli, seeded and chopped (optional)

Any or the following if available, chopped roughly (save
   your kitchen scraps): broccoli stems, cabbage outer
   leaves, cauliflower stems and leaves, leftover zucchini

10 cups water

1 tablespoon salt

*Place all ingredients in a large saucepan, cover, bring to the boil,
reduce heat and simmer gently for 1½ hours.*

Strain off liquid, discarding solids. Keep refrigerated.

Total cooking time: 15 minutes preparation, 1½ hours cooking
Makes: 1½ litres of stock

Chicken Stock

Protein

2 kg chicken bones

2 white onions and skins, finely chopped

3 sticks celery and leaves, chopped

1 cup parsley and stalks, chopped

3 bay leaves

4 stems rosemary

10 black peppercorns

12 cups water

1 tablespoon salt

Add all other ingredients to a large saucepan. Bring to the boil, reduce heat and simmer gently for 3 hours, skimming the top as it cooks.

Strain stock and discard solids. Keep refrigerated.

Total cooking time: 15 minutes preparation, 4 hours cooking
Makes: 1½ litres of stock

Fish Stock

Protein

1 kg fish bones, heads, tails, prawn shells

1 onion, finely chopped

2 sticks celery, sliced

1 teaspoon salt

1 teaspoon cracked black pepper

3 stems fresh rosemary

½ cup fresh basil, chopped

10 cups water

Put all ingredients into a large saucepan, cover, bring to the boil, reduce heat and simmer for 1 hour.

Remove from heat and strain to remove all solid material. Keep refrigerated.

Total cooking time: 15 minutes preparation, 1 hour cooking
Makes: 1½ litres of fish stock.

Red Curry Paste

Protein

6 fresh red chillies, chopped

5 white peppercorns

8 red shallots, peeled and sliced

6 lemon myrtle leaves, stems removed, finely chopped

2 stalks lemongrass, finely chopped

1 tablespoon galangal, peeled and chopped

2 cloves garlic, sliced

1 tablespoon chopped coriander root

1 teaspoon shrimp paste

1 teaspoon ground cumin

1 teaspoon paprika

1 teaspoon ground turmeric

60ml water

2 tablespoons basil leaves

1 cup peanut oil

Puree all ingredients together in a food processor. Heat a small saucepan and cook puree over medium heat for 30 minutes.

Keep refrigerated. Keeps for up to 1 month.

Total cooking time: 20 minutes preparation, 30 minutes cooking
Makes: 1½ cups of red curry paste

Green Curry Paste

Protein

8 small green chillies, seeded and chopped

3 cloves garlic, chopped

2 stalks fresh lemon grass, sliced

3 fresh coriander roots and stems, chopped

2 teaspoons grated lime rind

½ lime, juice

1 teaspoon caraway seeds

1 teaspoon ground turmeric

1 teaspoon shrimp paste

1 tablespoon water

Combine all ingredients in a food processor until a paste is formed.
Keep refrigerated. Keeps for up to 1 month.

Total cooking time: 20 minutes
Makes: 1 cup of green curry paste

Masaman Curry Paste

Carbohydrate/Protein

4 spring onions, finely chopped

2 cloves garlic, crushed

2 tablespoons fresh lemongrass, chopped

1 tablespoon dried red chillies, crushed

1 tablespoon coriander seeds

1 tablespoon cumin seeds

3 cardamom pods

½ teaspoon ground nutmeg

¼ teaspoon ground cloves

¼ teaspoon black peppercorns

2 teaspoons shrimp paste

2 tablespoons warm water

Combine all ingredients and process to form a paste. Keep refrigerated. Keeps for up to 1 month.

Total cooking time: 20 minutes preparation
Makes: ½ cup musaman curry paste

Salsa
Carbohydrate/Protein

This salsa is suitable for use with all carbohydrate and protein style meals. Use in salads and as a topping or garnish with meats.

3 large ripe tomatoes

1 medium red capsicum, seeded and finely chopped

1 red Spanish onion, minced

1 continental cucumber, seeded and finely chopped

4 tablespoons fresh parsley, finely chopped

2 tablespoons fresh basil leaves, finely chopped

1 red chilli, finely chopped

1 tablespoon lemon juice

1 tablespoon plain white vinegar

Salt and pepper to taste

Score bottom of each tomato with a cross. Drop into boiling water for 30 seconds, cool and peel. Seed and finely chop tomatoes.
Combine all ingredients together in a mixing bowl and mix well.
Keep refrigerated.

Total cooking time: 20 minutes preparation
Makes: 1½ cups of salsa

Pesto
Protein

Pesto is an excellent addition to any protein style meal. Use it to add flavour, texture and colour in your cooking.

¾ cup firmly packed fresh basil

¾ cup firmly packed fresh oregano

3 tablespoons parmesan cheese

¼ cup feta cheese, crumbled

4 tablespoons olive oil

2 cloves garlic, crushed

½ lemon, juice

1 teaspoon freshly cracked black pepper

Combine all ingredients in a food processor and blend well to form a paste.

Total cooking time: 20 minutes preparation
Makes: 1½ cups of pesto

Creamy Lemon Mayonnaise
Protein

This deliciously creamy mayonnaise with a hint of lemon, is excellent when tossed through a salad or poured over protein style meat, fish or vegetable dishes.

1 egg
1 egg yolk
½ teaspoon dried mustard powder
½ cup olive oil
½ cup cream
1 tablespoon lemon juice
1 teaspoon lemon zest

Lightly beat egg and yolk together, add dried mustard powder and mix well. Slowly pour olive oil into egg mixture, whisking well. Slowly pour cream into egg mixture, whisking well. Mix through lemon juice and zest.

Total cooking time: 10 minutes preparation
Makes: 1½ cups of mayonnaise.

Hollandaise Sauce
Protein

Traditional Hollandaise sauce is wonderful with roasted meat dishes and roasted vegetables.

4 egg yolks

2 tablespoons water

1 cup butter, melted

1 tablespoon lemon juice

Salt and pepper to season

Whisk egg yolks and water together over a very low heat for 2 minutes or until thick and foamy. Remove from heat. Slowly pour melted butter into the egg yolk mixture, whisking continually to form a thick and creamy sauce. Stir through lemon juice and seasoning. If sauce is runny, return to low heat and whisk until thickened. Try pouring Hollandaise sauce over your next roast with broccoli and cauliflower alfredo and steamed zucchini and baby yellow squash.

Total cooking time: 15 minutes preparation
Makes: 1 cup of hollandaise sauce.

Light Vinaigrette with Fresh Parsley and Roasted Garlic

Protein

1 head garlic, cloves separated and unpeeled

1½ cups fresh flat-leaf parsley

2 tablespoons lemon juice

2 tablespoons plain white vinegar

1 cup olive oil

Salt and pepper to season

Place garlic cloves on a baking tray in the oven for 20 minutes at 200°C. Once roasted, allow cloves to cool before peeling. In a food processor mince garlic and parsley with the lemon juice and white vinegar. Slowly add olive oil whilst whisking parsley and garlic puree vigorously. Season with salt and pepper. Serve over mixed salad or use as a dressing for any protein-style meal. Store in a glass jar in the refrigerator. You may need to warm the vinaigrette slightly before use, as it will solidify in the refrigerator.

Total cooking time: 20 minutes cooking, 15 minutes preparation
Makes: 2 cups of vinaigrette

Chilli Sauce
Carbohydrate/Protein

A South American style chilli sauce which can be used as a side dish or as a topping for any carbohydrate or protein style meal.

8 long green chillies

2 small yellow chillies

8 spring onions, trimmed and sliced

5 medium tomatoes

¼ cup fresh coriander leaves, finely chopped

1 teaspoon plain white vinegar

Salt and pepper to season

Place chillies under a hot grill and roast until skin blackens and blisters. Remove from grill, place in a plastic bag and allow to cool. Once cooled, remove skin, seed and finely chop.

Cut a cross through the bottom of each tomato, drop into boiling water for 30 seconds. Peel, seed and chop finely. Combine all ingredients and keep refrigerated. Use as a topping on any meal.

Total cooking time: 20 minutes grilling,15 minutes preparation
Makes: 2 cups of chilli sauce

Raita

Protein

Raita is typically served with Indian style dishes and hot curries.

1 onion, finely chopped
½ continental cucumber, peeled, seeded and diced finely
½ small fennel bulb, trimmed and finely chopped
250ml sour cream
1 tablespoon lemon juice
1 tablespoon plain white vinegar
2 tablespoons fresh dill, finely chopped
2 tablespoons fresh coriander, finely chopped
1 teaspoon caraway seeds
½ teaspoon cracked black peppercorns
1 teaspoon fennel seeds to garnish

Combine all ingredients, garnish with fennel seeds. Refrigerate overnight before serving. Serve with hot and spicy protein style meals.

Total cooking time: 15 minutes preparation
Makes: 2 cups of raita

Baba Ghanoush

Protein

Use this eggplant dip with celery, mushroom and cheese
dippers.

2 large eggplants
2 cloves garlic, crushed
3 tablespoons sour cream
2 tablespoons lemon juice
Salt and pepper to taste

*Place eggplants on a baking tray in the oven for 90 minutes at
200°C until softened and cooked through. Turn every so often. Allow
to cool before removing skin. Finely chop cooked eggplant flesh and
combine with other ingredients. Puree in a food processor. Serve as a
dip or sauce.*

Total cooking time: 90 minutes roasting, 10 minutes preparation
Makes: 2 cups of baba ghanoush

Hummus

Carbohydrate

220g dried chickpeas

1 onion, halved

2 bay leaves

3 cloves garlic, crushed

3 tablespoons lemon juice

   sweet potato, peeled and well cooked

   teaspoon ground cumin

Salt and pepper to taste

Soak chickpeas overnight. Half fill a saucepan with water and bring to the boil. Add chickpeas, onion and bay leaves. Simmer one hour or until chickpeas are cooked and very soft. Drain chickpeas, discard onion and bay leaves and reserve a few tablespoons of the cooking fluid. Combine chickpeas, garlic, lemon juice, sweet potato, cumin and seasoning in a food processor; puree. Add reserved cooking fluid if necessary to form a paste-like consistency. Serve as a dip, side-dish or topping with carbohydrate meals.

Total cooking time: 12 hours soaking, 1 hour cooking, 20 minutes preparation
Makes: 3 cups of hummus

Salmon Dip

Protein

1 pkt cured sliced salmon

1 block cream cheese, softened

½ cup cream

½ teaspoon cracked black pepper

Combine all ingredients in a food processor until well processed and pureed. Serve with protein style dippers and protein-style meals. I like to serve this dip with eggs. Hard boil two eggs; halve and scoop out the yolks. Combine yolks with 2 tablespoons of salmon dip to form a paste. With a piping tube squeeze egg yolk and salmon dip mixture onto the egg halves. Garnish with snipped chives. This is great as an entrée or snack.

Total cooking time: 5 minutes
Makes: 2 cups of salmon dip

Bacon and Onion Dip

Protein

1 tablespoon olive oil

6 rindless rashers bacon, chopped finely

1 large onion, chopped finely

½ cup sour cream

1 cup cream cheese, softened

2 tablespoons fresh chives, finely chopped

Salt and pepper to taste

Heat olive oil in a saucepan, fry bacon and onion until bacon is browned and onion softened. Combine sour cream and cream cheese in a food processor and blend well. Fold through bacon, onion, chives and seasoning. Serve with protein style dippers. You can also whisk an extra ½ cup of olive oil through this dip to use it as a dressing on mixed lettuce.

Total cooking time: 20 minutes preparation
Makes: 2 cups of bacon and onion dip

SNACKS

Spicy Roasted Chickpeas

Vegetable Crisps

Proscuitto Roll-Ups

Cheese and Sliced Meat

Fresh Vegetables

Semi-Sundried Tomatoes

Dolmades

Antipasto

Stuffed Eggs

Spicy Roasted Chickpeas
Carbohydrate

Roasted chickpeas can be used in place of peanuts as a snack. Also add roasted chickpeas to carbohydrate meals to give a crunchy texture and nutty flavor.

2 cups dried chickpeas

1 tablespoon tomato paste

1 tablespoon water

2 teaspoons salt

1 teaspoon pepper

1 teaspoon cayenne pepper

Rinse chickpeas then leave to soak for 24 hours. Drain, rinse and pat dry.

Combine chickpeas with all ingredients in a large mixing bowl. Spread chickpea mixture out onto a large baking tray. Place in the oven at 250°C for 40 minutes or until chickpeas are well roasted. Stir occasionally whilst baking. Allow to cool then season as desired.

Total cooking time: 24 hours soaking, 5 minutes preparation, 40 minutes cooking
Makes: 2 cups of roasted chickpeas

Vegetable Crisps
Protein

Oil for deep frying
4 small zucchinis, sliced very thinly lengthways
4 baby yellow squash, sliced very thinly
Salt and pepper to season

Heat oil to very hot in a large saucepan. Drop vegetables into oil a few at a time. Once browned and crisp remove from oil and allow to drain on paper towel. Season and serve. Use in place of potato crisps.

Total cooking time: 30 minutes

Prosciutto Roll-ups
Protein

This dish is great for hors d'oeuvre or entrées. You can vary this recipe to roll up any suitable ingredient you wish in the prosciutto slices

Slices of prosciutto
Chunks of brie, creamy blue or plain cream cheese
Caviar

Roll chunks of cheese and caviar up in prosciutto slices and serve.

Cheese and Sliced Meats
Protein

Cheese is an excellent protein snack. You can eat as much cheese as you like with any protein meal and between protein meals, such as for morning or afternoon tea. The only cheese not suitable is any cheese made with goats' milk or any cheese containing fruit, nuts, or poppy seeds. All the other cheeses you are free to enjoy. Incidentally parmesan cheese is your best source of calcium – better than milk.

Sliced meats are also an excellent snack which can be eaten with cheese. Once again you can eat as much meat as you like with any protein meal or between protein meals. You must avoid some processed sliced meats as they have sugar added or have been coated in sugar glaze or the like. Check with your deli assistant before you buy your sliced meat.

Always remember that cheese and sliced meats are protein in nature and therefore must not be eaten with carbohydrate meals. You should wait 3 hours after eating a carbohydrate meal before eating cheese and meat. You should wait 5 hours after eating cheese and meat before eating a carbohydrate meal.

Fresh Vegetables
Carbohydrate/Protein

The following vegetables can be eaten as snacks at any time of the day and with any type of meal, be it carbohydrate or protein. These vegetables are classified as excellent carbohydrates and therefore do not cause your blood sugar levels to rise. The glycemic index for these vegetables is below 20. Vegetables that are acceptable include mushrooms, celery, tomato, and cucumber. Have these fresh vegetables as snacks throughout the day or use with dips such as baba ghanoush or hummus.

Semi Sun-dried Tomatoes
Carbohydrate/Protein

Shop-bought sun-dried tomatoes can have added sugar and are usually placed in olive oil. Here is a suggestion for sun-dried tomatoes that are Glycemically correct.

Roma tomatoes
Vinegar
Mixed herbs

Slice tomatoes lengthways into quarters. Place on a lined baking tray in the oven at 200°C. Pour over a splash of vinegar and sprinkle with mixed herbs. Roast in the oven for approximately 30 minutes, or until semi-dried. Serve with dips, as an ingredient for brochette, or with an antipasto dish.

Dolmades
Carbohydrate

Vine leaves
1 cup of basmati rice
2 tablespoons lemon juice
2 cups of water
salt and pepper

Boil rice until nearly cooked. Drain and set aside to cool. In a bowl combine cooled rice, lemon juice, salt and pepper. In a colander, separate vine leaves, and allow to drain off excess brine. On a flat surface place vine leaf with shiny side down. If the vine leaf is small or thin add an extra leaf to give it strength. Place a small amount of rice mixture in the middle of each leaf. Fold in each side and carefully roll up. When all the rice has been used, place the dolmades in a bowl side by side, as tightly packed as possible. Place a weight on top of the dolmades to prevent them unravelling, then pour 2 cups of cold water over. Place in a moderate oven and cook until vine leaves are soft. Serve with Quick Napoli Sauce (see main meals section) as a hot meal. Or serve cold as a starter.

Makes approximately 30 dolmades.

Antipasto

Carbohydrate

This dish is rather versatile, and can be served as a starter, entrée, side dish, or main meal. Antipasto can also be served with, or as, a protein meal when bread is not included.

2 medium red capsicums

1 medium eggplant

1 medium zucchini

1 can artichoke hearts

4 roma tomatoes

1 tablespoon dried oregano

Salt and pepper

Slice capsicums in half and remove seeds, then cut into 1cm slices lengthways. Remove top of eggplant, cut eggplant in half, then slice into thin slices lengthways. Prepare zucchini in a similar fashion. Place on a lined tray beneath a griller. Season with salt, pepper, and oregano. Grill until brown.

Drain artichokes, slice in half. Also slice tomatoes in half lengthways, once the ends have been removed. Place artichokes and tomatoes on a lined tray in an oven at 200°C, and bake until well roasted.

Once prepared, arrange all vegetables on a serving platter Serve as an entrée or as a side dish. To serve as a protein style antipasto, simply add some sliced meats and cheeses to the platter.

Stuffed Eggs
Protein

This is a tasty and easy-to-prepare recipe for serving as a starter, or when entertaining at parties or functions.

12 small eggs
1 tablespoon mayonnaise (as above)
1 tablespoon sour lite cream
1 teaspoon Australian mustard (no added sugar)

Hard boil eggs. Place in a bowl of cold water for one hour. Remove egg shells and cut in half lengthways. Remove yolks and combine with other ingredients into a smooth creamy consistency. Spoon or pipe mixture back into egg halves. Decorate as desired with caviar, smoked salmon, asparagus, radish, cherry tomatoes and herbs.

SOUPS

Cauliflower and Cream Cheese Soup

Fresh Tomato Soup with Chickpeas and Rosemary

Seafood Chowder

Creamy Asparagus Soup

Sweet Potato and Lentil Soup with Coriander

Vietnamese Style Spicy Seafood Soup

Hearty Vegetable Soup

Creamy Mushroom Soup

Curried Cream of Chicken Soup

Original Tomato Soup

Bok Choy and Tofu Soup

Eggplant and Leek Soup

Bacon, Cabbage and Cauliflower Soup

Cauliflower and Cream Cheese Soup

Protein

An excellent soup to serve with any protein meal, its subtle flavour and texture giving renewed popularity to this sometimes disregarded vegetable.

1 medium head cauliflower, cut into small florets

3 cups chicken stock

220g cream cheese

¾ cup cream

¾ teaspoon ground nutmeg

Salt and pepper to taste

Fresh chervil to garnish

Bring stock and cauliflower to the boil in a large saucepan. Reduce heat and simmer for 20 minutes or until cauliflower is soft. Process stock and cauliflower with cream cheese in a blender until smooth. Return cauliflower puree to the saucepan. Add cream, nutmeg and seasoning. Heat through and serve garnished with fresh chervil.

Total cooking time: 40 minutes
Serves: 4 large soup bowls

Fresh Tomato Soup with Chickpeas and Rosemary

Carbohydrate

A deliciously fresh tomato soup, with the chickpeas and rosemary adding aroma and flavour to create a warm and hearty meal.

8 spring onions, trimmed and sliced
2 cloves garlic, crushed
2 tablespoons fresh rosemary, chopped finely
4 large tomatoes, peeled and diced
4 cups vegetable stock
1½ cups cooked chickpeas (or 400g can chickpeas drained – no added sugar)
Salt and pepper to taste
Extra sprigs of fresh rosemary to garnish

Heat a large saucepan, add spring onions and garlic with 2 tablespoons of water and sauté until softened. Add tomatoes and rosemary to onion and garlic. Stir-fry 5 minutes over medium heat. Add stock, chickpeas and seasoning to tomato and onion mixture, bring to the boil, reduce heat and simmer for 20 minutes. Serve garnished with a sprig of fresh rosemary.

Total cooking time: 35 minutes
Serves: 4 large soup bowls

Seafood Chowder
Protein

A wonderful combination of fish, prawns and pipis in a creamy bacon and peppercorn soup, perfect for a seaside luncheon.

500g fresh pipis in the shell
¾ cup water
500g white fish, skinned, boned and cut into 2cm pieces
8 king green prawns, peeled and deveined
2 tablespoons butter
1 large onion, finely chopped
2 bay leaves
2 tablespoons of parsley, chopped
2 tablespoons thyme, chopped
10 black peppercorns
3 cups water, extra
1 tablespoon butter, extra
4 rashers bacon, finely chopped
1 leek, trimmed and sliced
1 stick celery, finely sliced
1 cup cream
4 tablespoons fresh parsley, finely chopped, extra
Salt and pepper to taste
Extra parsley to garnish

Place pipis in a large saucepan with ¾ cup water, cover and simmer 5 minutes or until shells are opened. Discard any shells that do not open. Strain liquid and reserve. Remove meat from shells, discard shells and chop meat finely.

Prepare fish and prawns, reserve trimmings, bones and shells, set aside.

Heat 2 tablespoons of butter in a large saucepan, add reserved trimmings, bones and shells and onion, stir-fry 3 minutes. Add reserved fluid from cooking the pipis, bay leaves, parsley, thyme, peppercorns and the extra 3 cups of water. Bring to the boil, reduce heat and simmer 30 minutes, skimming the top of the soup as it cooks. When done, strain off fluid stock and reserve. Discard solids.

Add extra butter to a large wok and heat. Add bacon, leek and celery, stir-fry 3 minutes. Add reserved stock and fish, heat 5 minutes. Add pipi meat, prawns, cream, parsley and seasoning. Heat through an extra five minutes or until prawns change colour. Serve garnished with parsley.

Total cooking time: 45 minutes
Serves: 4 large soup bowls

Creamy Asparagus Soup
Protein

Rich in folate and vitamins, asparagus creates a distinctive creamy soup.

1 small onion, chopped

1 stick celery, chopped

1 tablespoon butter

16 spears asparagus, chopped

2½ cups chicken stock

½ cup cream

1½ tablespoon snipped fresh chives

Salt and pepper to taste

Extra cream and chives to garnish

Heat butter in a large saucepan. Add onion and celery and fry 5 minutes until onion is soft. Add stock and asparagus, bring to the boil, reduce heat and simmer for 30 minutes or until asparagus is very soft. Process stock and asparagus in a blender until smooth. Return asparagus puree to saucepan. Add cream, chives and seasoning. Blend and heat gently until warmed through.
Serve garnished with a dollop of cream and fresh chives.

Total cooking time: 40 minutes
Serves: 4 large soup bowls

Sweet Potato and Lentil Soup with Coriander

Carbohydrate

A thick and hearty soup with a hint of spice. Suitable for freezing.

1 large onion, sliced

1 clove garlic, crushed

6 cups vegetable stock

2 medium orange sweet potatoes, peeled and diced

250g red lentils

   teaspoon dried chilli flakes

   teaspoon all spice

Salt and pepper to taste

   cup fresh coriander chopped

Sauté onion and garlic in a large non-stick saucepan with 2 tablespoons of water, until soft. Add stock, sweet potato, lentils, chilli and allspice, bring to the boil, reduce heat and simmer 30 minuter or until potato is soft. Puree potato and lentils in a food processor. Stir through seasoning and coriander.

Total cooking time: 40 minutes
Serves: 4 large soup bowls

Vietnamese Style Spicy Seafood Soup
Protein

1½ cups Chinese dried sliced mushrooms

250g fresh white fish fillets, trimmed and cubed

8 king green prawns, shelled and deveined, tails left
intact

1 prepared calamari hood, sliced

2 tablespoons peanut oil

1 teaspoon sesame oil

3 kaffir lime leaves

1 clove garlic, crushed

1 teaspoon ginger chopped

1 red chilli, seeded and chopped

1 whole lemon, sliced

6 cups water

1 tablespoon fish sauce

3 choy sum (Chinese broccoli), trimmed and chopped

3 bok choy, trimmed and chopped

8 cherry tomatoes, halved

¼ cup fresh coriander, chopped

Fresh bamboo shoots, chopped red chilli and lemon
wedges to garnish

Place sliced mushrooms in boiling hot water and leave to soak 30 minutes. Prepare fish, prawns and calamari. Reserve shells and trimmings.

To a large wok add oils then heat. Add seafood shells and trimmings, lime leaves, garlic, ginger, chilli and sliced lemon. Stir-fry 2 minutes. Add 6 cups of water to the wok and bring to the boil, reduce heat and simmer uncovered for 30 minutes, skimming the top of as it cooks. Strain seafood stock and discard solids.

Return stock to wok and add prawns, fish, calamari, mushrooms, fish sauce and choy sum. Bring to the boil, reduce heat and simmer 3 minutes or until prawns change colour and fish is tender. Add bok choy and tomatoes, simmer 1 minute more. Stir through coriander and serve garnished with bamboo shoots, chopped red chilli and lemon wedges.

Total cooking time: 30 minutes
Serves: 4 large soup bowls

Hearty Vegetable Soup
Carbohydrate

This chunky vegetable soup can be served as a meal in itself.
This soup is suitable for vegetarians and vegans.

1 leek, trimmed, halved lengthways and sliced

1 large onion, sliced

2 celery sticks, sliced

1 large zucchini, chopped

4 yellow squash, chopped

1 large eggplant, peeled and chopped

1½ tablespoons tomato paste

6 cups vegetable stock

2 medium sweet potatoes, peeled and chopped

¾ cup cooked red kidney beans

2 tablespoons fresh parsley, finely chopped

Salt and pepper to taste

Sauté leek and onion in a large saucepan with 2 tablespoons of water until soft. Add celery, zucchini, squash and eggplant to the saucepan and cook for 5 minutes. Add tomato paste and cook for a further minute. Add stock and sweet potato to the saucepan, bring to the boil, reduce heat and simmer 15 minutes. Add red kidney beans, parsley and seasoning. Simmer a further 10 minutes or until sweet potato is soft.

Total cooking time: 40 minutes
Serves: 4 large soup bowls

Creamy mushroom soup
Protein

A wonderful winter soup, made with lovely fresh mushrooms.

4 tablespoons butter

500g mushrooms, peeled and roughly chopped

1 clove garlic, crushed

4 cups chicken stock

1 cup cream

¾ teaspoon all-spice

1 tablespoon fresh parsley, finely chopped

Salt and pepper to taste

Sour cream and fresh parsley to garnish

Melt butter in a large saucepan, add mushrooms and garlic and cook for 5 minutes or until mushrooms are soft. Add stock to mushrooms and bring to the boil, reduce heat and simmer for 15 minutes. Process mushrooms and stock in a blender until smooth. Return mushroom puree to the saucepan, add cream, all-spice, parsley and seasoning and heat through. Serve garnished with a dollop of sour cream and sprigs of fresh parsley.

Total cooking time: 30 minutes
Serves: 4 large soup bowls

Curried cream of chicken soup
Protein

A wholesome chicken soup with plenty of curry to keep
you warm.

2 tablespoons peanut oil

4 tablespoons red curry paste

3 chicken breast fillets, chopped roughly

4 cups chicken stock

2 egg yolks

250g cream cheese, softened

1 cup cream

12 cherry tomatoes, halved

1 bunch fresh coriander leaves, chopped

Salt and pepper to taste

Extra coriander to garnish

*Heat peanut oil in a large wok, add curry paste and chicken and
stir-fry 10 minutes or until chicken is browned and cooked through.
Remove chicken from the wok and finely chop. Meanwhile, combine
egg yolks, cream cheese and cream in a food processor until smooth and
well blended. Bring stock to the boil in a large saucepan, stir through
egg, cheese and cream mixture; add chicken and heat gently. Add
cherry tomatoes, coriander and seasoning and mix through. Serve
garnished with extra coriander.*

Total cooking time: 30 minutes
Serves: 4 large soup bowls

Original tomato soup
Carbohydrate

You can't beat the original tomato soup, it's everyone's favourite.

12 tomatoes, peeled

1 large sweet potato, peeled and diced

1 large onion, finely chopped

2 cloves garlic, crushed

3 cups vegetable stock

2 cups tomato juice (no added sugar)

¼ cup fresh parsley, finely chopped

¼ cup fresh basil, finely chopped

1 tablespoon fresh rosemary, finely chopped

Salt and pepper to taste

Heat a large saucepan, add onion and garlic with 1 tablespoon of water, sauté until onion is soft. Add stock, tomato juice, tomatoes, sweet potato, herbs and seasoning, bring to the boil, reduce heat and simmer 30 minutes or until sweet potato is soft. Puree soup in a processor. Serve garnished with parsley.

Total cooking time: 40 minutes
Serves: 4 large soup bowls

Bok Choy and Tofu Soup
Carbohydrate

This is Asian style soup will keep you warm in winter. The larger metropolitan supermarkets sell dried beancurd; it is also readily available in Asian supermarkets.

½ packet dried bean curd
½ bunch fresh coriander
½ bunch fresh Vietnamese mint
2 cups fresh bean shoots
1 cup dried fungus
1 can straw mushrooms (no added sugar)
1 tablespoon fish sauce (no added sugar)
1 small chilli, seeded and chopped
1 tablespoon tamarind puree
1 clove garlic, crushed
1 tablespoon ginger, grated
2 bunches of bok choy, washed and trimmed
5 cups of water
salt to taste

In a hot, non-stick saucepan, fry cubed bean curd, garlic, ginger and chilli. Add 1 cup of water, fish sauce, dried fungus, drained straw mushrooms, and tamarind puree. Allow to boil, then add remaining water and reduce until fungus is soft. Add bok choy leaves to soup and allow to wilt before serving topped with handfuls of fresh coriander, Vietnamese mint and bean shoots.

Total cooking time: 40 minutes
Serves: 4

Eggplant and Leek Soup
Carbohydrate

We have added a variation to this soup to give it a creamier texture if desired, simply by adding a can of chickpeas (drained and no added sugar).

2 medium eggplants, peeled and diced
2 leeks, sliced
5 cups vegetable stock
salt and pepper
½ teaspoon nutmeg
fresh parsley

Place eggplant and leek in a hot non-stick fry pan with a small amount of water, fry until leek softens. Heat stock in a large saucepan, add eggplant and leek, seasoning and spice, bring to boil then allow to simmer covered until eggplant is soft and cooked through. Serve soup in bowls topped with chopped fresh parsley. Variation: Add 1 can of drained, vitamised chickpeas to the soup when the eggplant is soft and cooked through. Heat soup until hot once again, then serve as suggested with fresh parsley on top.

Total cooking time: 30 minutes
Serves: 4

Bacon, Cabbage and Cauliflower Soup

Protein

1 tablespoon butter

6 rashers of rindless bacon, chopped

2 leeks, sliced

2 cloves of garlic, crushed

½ medium cauliflower, cut into floretes

½ medium cabbage, shredded

5 chicken stock

salt and pepper

2 spring onions, chopped

dollop of sour cream

sweet paprika

Heat butter in a large saucepan, add bacon, leek and garlic, sauté 5 minutes. Add chicken stock, cabbage, cauliflower and seasoning, bring to the boil, simmer with lid off for 30 minutes. Serve with a dollop of sour cream, chopped spring onions, and a sprinkle of sweet paprika.

Total cooking time: 40 minutes
Serves: 4

SALADS

Warm Red Curry Chicken with Salsa Verde

Turkish Tabouli Salad with Red Lentils

Marinated Haloumi with Roma Tomatoes and Spinach

Mexican Capsicum and Bean Salad

Basmati Rice Salad

Roasted Vegetable Salad with Salsa

Traditional Caesar Salad

Warm Thai Beef Salad

Squid and Octopus Salad

Tuna and Vegetable Salad

Warm Red Curry Chicken Salad with Salsa Verde

Protein

A taste bud extravaganza; whoever said eating healthy food was boring?

2 large ripe tomatoes, seeded and chopped

1 cup fresh parsley, finely chopped

6 anchovies fillets, mashed

1 lemon, juice

½ cup olive oil

½ teaspoon cracked black pepper

1 tablespoon olive oil, extra

3 chicken breast fillets, skin off, sliced thickly

1½ tablespoon red curry paste

4 tablespoons sour cream

4 cups mixed lettuce leaves

Combine tomatoes, parsley, anchovies, lemon juice, olive oil and pepper. Mix well and set aside. Heat olive oil in a large fry pan. Add chicken slices and fry until golden brown and cooked through. Add red curry paste and stir-fry a further 2 minutes. Add sour cream and stir-fry a further minute. Arrange mixed lettuce onto four plates, pile chicken slices on top of salad and spoon over salsa verde.

Total cooking time: 25 minutes
Serves: 4

Turkish Tabouli Salad with Red Lentils

Carbohydrate

This salad offers all the flavour of the Middle East, providing a full wholesome meal in itself. You may also wish to serve this as a side-dish or with a salsa or chilli sauce.

1½ cups coarse bulgur (cracked wheat)

1½ cups red lentils

8 spring onions, trimmed and sliced

2 large tomatoes, seeded and diced

1 red capsicum, seeded and diced

1 continental cucumber, seeded and diced

1 cup fresh parsley, finely chopped

¼ cup fresh mint, chopped

2 lemons, juice

½ teaspoon hot chilli powder

2 teaspoons ground cumin

2 tablespoons tomato paste (no added sugar)

Salt and pepper to taste

Rinse bulgur and lentils well. Place in a bowl full of water, leave to soak 24 hours. Drain well and pat dry. Add all other ingredients to the bulgur and lentils and mix well. Keep covered and refrigerated.

Total cooking time: 15 minutes preparation, 12 hours soaking
Serves: 6

Marinated Haloumi with Roma Tomatoes and Spinach

Protein

220g haloumi cheese, cut into 1 cm slices

2 cloves garlic, chopped

1 tablespoon fresh oregano, chopped

1 tablespoon fresh marjoram, chopped

1 cup olive oil

8 Roma tomatoes, halved lengthways

2 red Spanish onions, ends intact, cut into wedges

2 tablespoons olive oil, extra

315g (10oz) baby spinach leaves

Place haloumi slices in a baking dish, scatter over garlic and fresh herbs. Pour over olive oil and allow to marinade 2-3 hours. Grease a baking dish with extra olive oil, add tomatoes and onions. Bake in oven at 200°C for 1 hour. Remove haloumi from the marinade and place under a hot grill. Grill each side 10 minutes or until golden brown. Wash spinach thoroughly; divide between four plates. Arrange tomato, onion and haloumi on top of spinach. Drizzle a little of the marinade over each salad. Serve.

Total cooking time: 3 hours marinating, 1 hour cooking, 10 minutes preparation
Serves: 4

Mexican Capsicum and Bean Salad
Carbohydrate

A spicy bean salad fit for a Mexican.

1 red Spanish onion, chopped

2 cloves garlic, minced

2 small green chillies, seeded and chopped

2 red capsicums, seeded and chopped

1 green capsicum, seeded and chopped

1 yellow capsicum, seeded and chopped

1 tablespoon paprika

6 yellow squash, chopped

1 tablespoon ground cumin

1 cup cooked lima beans

1 cup cooked red kidney beans

1 teaspoon Tabasco sauce

2 limes, juice

¾ cup fresh coriander leaves, chopped

Salt and pepper to taste

Heat a large non-stick fry pan, add onion, garlic and chillies with 1 tablespoon of water. Cook 5 minutes or until onion is soft. Add capsicum, squash, paprika, cumin and 2 tablespoons of water. Cook 15 minutes or until vegetables are well browned and cooked through. Remove from heat. Add lima beans, red kidney beans, Tabasco, lime juice, coriander and seasoning. Mix well. Serve.

Total cooking time: 30 minutes
Serves: 6

Basmati Rice Salad
Carbohydrate

This carbohydrate style salad can be served as a meal in itself or as a side-dish. It is very convenient for taking as a packed lunch to work.

1½ cups yellow lentils

1½ cups basmati rice

315g cannelloni or Soya beans, cooked

4 large ripe tomatoes, seeded and chopped

1 continental cucumber, seeded and chopped

2 tablespoons fresh oregano leaves, finely chopped

½ cup basil leaves, finely chopped

1 tablespoon garlic chives, finely chopped

1 lemon, juice

1 tablespoon plain white vinegar

Salt and pepper to taste

Soak and cook lentils as per instructions on packaging. Allow to cool. Cook basmati rice, drain and allow to cool. Combine all ingredients in a large mixing bowl, mix well and serve.

Total cooking time: 12 hours soaking, 30 minutes cooking
Serves: 4

Roasted Vegetable Salad with Salsa

Carbohydrate

2 medium sweet potatoes, peeled and chunked

2 zucchini, trimmed and quartered

220g mushrooms, peeled, stalks removed

4 yellow squash, trimmed and quartered

2 small eggplants, trimmed and sliced 1cm thick

2 tablespoons tomato paste (no added sugar)

2 large red capsicums, seeded and quartered

4 artichoke hearts, halved (use canned artichoke hearts)

1 small broccoli, divided into florets

Salt and pepper to taste

Salsa to serve

Boil sweet potatoes until they begin to soften. Drain and transfer to a baking tray with zucchini, mushrooms, yellow squash and eggplant. Mix tomato paste with 2 tablespoons of water, baste vegetables. Cook vegetables 50 minutes at 180°C or until browned and well cooked. Remove from oven and allow to cool.

Grill capsicum until skin is blackened and blistered. Allow to cool then remove skin. Steam broccoli florets 3 minutes so that they retain their crispness and color. Combine all vegetables then arrange onto four plates, sprinkle with fresh parsley and seasoning. Serve topped with salsa.

Total cooking time: 1 hour 10 minutes
Serves: 4

Traditional Caesar Salad
Protein

An old favourite, this salad is always sure to please.

2 cos lettuces

4 rashers rindless bacon, chopped

1 tablespoon olive oil

1 small tin anchovies

125g block parmesan cheese, shaved

½ cup olive oil, extra

4 tablespoons sour cream

Oil from anchovies tin

1 clove garlic, crushed

2 eggs, boiled 1 minute

½ teaspoon Tabasco sauce

½ teaspoon mustard powder

½ lemon, juice

Salt and pepper to taste

6 hardboiled eggs, halved

Extra shaved parmesan to garnish

Separate lettuce leaves and rinse thoroughly, discarding any discoloured or wilted leaves. In four serving bowls arrange 4 leaves per bowl around outside of bowl. Chop remaining leaves in half and lengthways and place in a large mixing bowl.

Heat 1 tablespoon of olive oil in a frypan and cook bacon until crisp and browned. Mix bacon, 12 anchovies and shaved parmesan through chopped lettuce.

In a small bowl combine extra olive oil, sour cream, anchovy oil, garlic, runny eggs, Tabasco sauce, mustard powder, lemon juice and seasoning, whisk to combine well. Pour dressing over lettuce, bacon and anchovies. Divide lettuce mixture amongst bowls, ensuring that whole lettuce leaves remain to the outside of the bowl. Place boiled eggs on top and garnish with extra parmesan cheese.

Total cooking time: 30 minutes
Serves: 4

Warm Thai Beef Salad
Protein

This recipe brings together some interesting Asian ingredients to add flavour, variety and interest to your home cooked meals.

1 red chilli, seeded and minced

2 teaspoons black pepper

1 teaspoon grated lime zest

500g lean beef steak, trimmed of fat

1 tablespoon ghee or butter

250g shitake mushrooms

250g oyster mushrooms

¼ cup chicken or vegetable stock

1 lime juice

1 tablespoon fish sauce

½ continental cucumber, sliced

4 spring onions, thinly sliced

1 cup fresh Thai or sweet basil leaves, chopped

½ cup fresh mint leaves, chopped

fresh coriander leaves to garnish

Place chilli, pepper and lime zest in a mortar and grind to form a coarse paste. Rub paste over meat. Brown meat under the grill 1–2 minutes on each side; beef should be rare. Allow to stand 10 minutes before slicing thinly; set aside.

Heat ghee in a wok over medium heat, add mushrooms and stir-fry 5 minutes. Add stock, lime juice and fish sauce, bring to the boil then remove from heat. Mix meat, mushroom mixture, cucumber, basil and mint. Pile onto plates and garnish with coriander.

Total cooking time: 25 minutes
Serves: 4

Squid and Octopus Salad
Protein

Use fresh squid and octopus from a fishmonger for this recipe. This dish is excellent for entertaining.

1 kg squid, cleaned

1 kg octopus, cleaned

salt and pepper

2 bay leaves

6 peppercorns

30g butter

1 small onion, finely chopped

350ml olive oil

2 large tomatoes, chopped

4 tablespoons vinegar

3 tablespoons chopped fresh parsley

3 tablespoons snipped fresh chives

2 cloves of garlic peeled and halved

1 cos lettuce

1 curly endive

½ cup of olive oil

½ cup of white vinegar

2 tablespoons of lemon juice

6 cherry tomatoes

chopped parsley

Cook octopus in a large saucepan of water with salt, pepper, bay leaves and peppercorns until tender (1-2 hours depending on the size of the octopus). Allow to cool in water then cut into bite size pieces.

Cut squid into julienne pieces. Add to a hot fry pan with melted butter and stir-fry until squid turns opaque; set aside to cool.

Sauté onions and tomatoes in a hot fry pan, allow to cool then add olive oil, vinegar, parsley, chives, garlic, octopus and squid. Place mixture in a covered container in the refrigerator overnight.

Wash and dry cos lettuce and endive. Place in a large bowl and mix through with a vinaigrette of olive oil, vinegar, lemon juice, salt and pepper. Pile salad onto six plates. Spoon squid and octopus mixture on top of lettuce. Garnish with cherry tomatoes and parsley.

Total cooking time: 20 minutes cooking, 12 hours marinating, 10 minutes preparation
Serves: 6

Tuna and Vegetable Salad

Protein

125g green beans, trimmed

4 cups mixed lettuce

1 medium tomato, cut into segments

½ red onion, sliced

2 hard boiled eggs, halved

1 large can of tuna in spring water

8 anchovies

2 tablespoons olive oil

1 tablespoons white vinegar

1 clove of garlic, crushed

1 tblsp of Australian mustard (no added sugar)

Blanch beans in a large saucepan of boiling water for 30 seconds, then drain and flush with cold water until completely cooled; let drain. Divide lettuce between four plates and arrange beans, segments of tomato, quarters of egg, chunks of tuna and anchovies on top.
In a small jar combine olive oil, white vinegar, garlic and mustard. Shake well and drizzle over salad.

Total cooking time: 15 minutes
Serves: 4

SIDE DISHES

Stir-Fried Chinese Vegetables
Coleslaw with Coriander and Chilli
Indian Style Vegetables
Broccoli and Cauliflower Alfredo
Cabbage Noodles
Asparagus and Salmon with Hollandaise Sauce
Marinated Feta Cheese and Mushrooms
Blanched Green Vegetables with Light Vinaigrette
Lemon and Herbed Basmati Rice
Tabouli

Stir Fried Chinese Vegetables

Carbohydrate/Protein

This side-dish is suitable with all carbohydrate and protein style meals.

315g green string beans, cut into 10 cm pieces

1 bunch Chinese broccoli, cut into 10 cm pieces

8 spring onions, sliced

2 cloves garlic, crushed

2 teaspoons fresh ginger, grated

1 red chilli, seeded and chopped

1 bunch English spinach leaves, trimmed and washed

2 bunches baby bok choy, trimmed and washed

1 tablespoon lime juice

¼ cup fresh coriander leaves, chopped

salt to taste

Blanch beans and broccoli. Heat a large wok and add a little water with the onion, garlic, ginger and chilli. Stir-fry 3 minutes. Add all other ingredients to the wok and stir-fry briefly to heat through until spinach has just wilted.

Total cooking time: 20 minutes
Serves: 6 side-dish servings

Coleslaw with Coriander and Chilli

Protein

1 red chilli, seeded and chopped

1 cup fresh coriander leaves, chopped

2 cloves garlic, crushed

2 tablespoons fresh mint leaves, chopped

1 lime, juice and zest

4 tablespoons sour cream

4 tablespoons olive oil

Salt and pepper to taste

½ green cabbage, chopped

½ red cabbage, chopped

1 red Spanish onion, sliced

Combine chilli, coriander, garlic, mint, lime juice and zest, sour cream, olive oil and seasoning in a food processor. Place in covered container in refrigerator and leave overnight. Combine green and red cabbage and onion, mix through coriander and chilli dressing and serve.

Total cooking time: 12 hours refrigeration, 15 minutes preparation
Serves: 6 side-dish servings

Indian Style Vegetables

Protein

2 tablespoons peanut oil

1 tablespoon sesame oil

1 tablespoon red curry paste

1 large onion, sliced

8 baby yellow squash, sliced

1 green capsicum sliced

1 yellow capsicum sliced

20 button mushrooms, quartered

2 small zucchinis, sliced

Salt to taste

Heat oils in a large wok, add all other ingredients and stir-fry 8 minutes over high heat until soft and cooked through. Season.

Total cooking time: 15 minutes
Serves: 6 side-dish servings

Broccoli and Cauliflower Alfredo
Protein

½ head broccoli, cut into florets

½ head cauliflower, cut into florets

1 egg

4 tablespoons cream cheese, softened

2 tablespoons cream

2 tablespoons grated parmesan cheese

Salt and pepper to season

½ cup grated tasty cheese

¾ teaspoon nutmeg

Steam vegetables until just cooked. Combine egg, cream cheese, cream and parmesan cheese. Stir cheese mixture through vegetables until they are well coated in sauce. Place vegetables in a large casserole dish, season and sprinkle with tasty cheese and nutmeg. Place under a grill for 10 minutes or until cheese is melted and beginning to brown.

Total cooking time: 20 minutes
Serves: 6 side-dish servings

Cabbage Noodles
Protein

Cabbage noodles are excellent for serving with a protein style
Napolese sauce. Try stir-frying minced meat, onion and garlic;
add tomato paste, tomatoes and mixed herbs and seasoning;
simmer to thicken then pour the sauce over the cabbage
noodles.

1 cabbage, shredded
4 tablespoons butter
Salt and pepper to season

Melt butter in a large saucepan, add cabbage and sauté 5 minutes.
Season and serve.

Total cooking time: 10 minutes
Serves: 6 side-dish servings

Asparagus and Salmon with Hollandaise Sauce

Protein

Excellent as a side-dish, entrée or even for breakfast.

16 asparagus spears, trimmed
1 pkt sliced salmon
Cracked black peppercorns to season
½ cup Hollandaise sauce

Blanch asparagus spears in salted water until just softened and cooked. Wrap two spears of asparagus together with one piece of salmon, just around the mid-section of the asparagus. Arrange asparagus onto plates, season and pour over Hollandaise sauce.

Total cooking time: 15 minutes
Serves: 4 side-dish servings

Marinated Feta Cheese and Mushrooms
Protein

3 cloves garlic, crushed

1 cup olive oil

1 tablespoon lemon juice

1 teaspoon chilli flakes

½ cup fresh parsley, finely chopped

250g feta cheese, sliced thickly

250g button mushrooms, peeled, stalks removed

Combine garlic, olive oil, lemon juice, chilli and parsley. Pour marinade over feta cheese and mushrooms. Place in a covered container in the refrigerator for at least 12 hours before serving. Serve as a side dish with protein-style meals, or as an antipasto type snack.

Total cooking time: 10 minutes preparation, 12 hours marinating
Serves: 4 side-dish servings

Blanched Green Vegetables with Light Vinaigrette

Protein

15 long green beans, trimmed and halved

½ head broccoli, florets

1 large zucchini, sliced on the diagonal

½ cup light vinaigrette with fresh parsley and
roasted garlic

Blanch vegetables in boiling water so they are cooked but remain crisp. Place in a large mixing bowl and mix through vinaigrette. Divide between four plates and serve.

Total cooking time: 15 minutes
Serves: 4 side-dish servings

Lemon and Herbed Basmati Rice

Carbohydrate

1 cup basmati rice

1 tablespoon lemon juice

2 tablespoons fresh coriander, chopped

Boil rice until soft and cooked through; drain. Stir through lemon juice and coriander and serve with any carbohydrate style dish. You may wish to substitute the coriander for any other fresh herbs that you have available such as dill, mint or coriander.

Total cooking time: 20 minutes
Serves: 4 side-dish servings

Tabouli

Carbohydrate

This is a Lebanese style salad excellent for serving with Dolmades.

1 large bunch of fresh curly parsley
½ cup of boughul wheat
2 cups of water
4 tablespoon of lemon juice
2 spring onions
1 large tomato
salt and pepper

In a medium bowl soak boughul wheat in water until it is absorbed (approximately 1 hour). Remove leaves of parsley from stems, wash and drain well. Finely chop parsley and combine with lemon juice, finely chop tomato and spring onions. Drain boughul wheat of any excess water and stir through parsley and tomato mixture. Season with salt and pepper.

Total cooking time: 1 hour 20 minutes preparation
Serves: 4 side-dish servings

Baked Ricotta with Semi Sundried Tomatoes

Protein

This recipe can be served as an entrée, after dinner cheese platter or simply as a snack between protein meals.

1 round fresh ricotta

2 cloves garlic, crushed

1 lemon, juice and zest

155g semi-dried tomatoes, roughly chopped

1 cup fresh flat-leaf parsley, finely chopped

1 cup fresh coriander leaves, chopped

⅓ cup olive oil

Place ricotta on a greased baking tray and bake at 250°C for 30 minutes. Combine other ingredients and serve spooned over slices of ricotta. Serve with appropriate protein-style side-dish.

Total cooking time: 35 minutes
Serves: 4-6

RISOTTOS AND PILAUS

Barley Pilau

Chickpeas and Rice

Indian Style Red Lentil Pilau

Spicy Roasted Vegetable Paella with Chickpeas

Risotto with Fresh Dill and Roasted Tomato Wedges

Barley Pilau

Carbohydrate

1½ cups dried sliced Chinese mushrooms

8 spring onions, trimmed and sliced

2 cloves garlic, crushed

1 tablespoon fresh ginger, grated

1 teaspoon sichuan peppercorns, crushed

1½ cups pearled barley

3 cups vegetable stock

2 choy sum (Chinese broccoli), cut into 5cm lengths

Salt to taste

*Soak mushrooms in hot water for 30 minutes. Drain and reserve
½ cup of the fluid. Set aside.*

*To a large non-stick saucepan add spring onions, garlic, ginger and
2 tablespoons of water. Stir-fry 2 minutes or until onion is soft. Add
peppercorns and barley, stir-fry 3 minutes or until barley begins to
brown. Add mushrooms, reserved fluid and stock, bring to the boil,
reduce heat and simmer covered for 30 minutes or until barley has
softened and liquid absorbed. Cook off any excess liquid by stir-frying
uncovered.*

*Steam choy sum for 3 minutes so that it remains crisp. Stir choy sum
and seasoning through barley pilau. Serve.*

Total cooking time: 1 hour
Serves: 6

Chickpeas and Rice
Carbohydrate

This is a good dish for serving with other carbohydrate meals, particularly with a vegetable curry. Once again canned chickpeas can be used as long as they have no added sugar. Basmati rice should be used.

½ cup of dried chickpeas

2 medium onions, sliced

2 cloves of garlic, crushed

1 fresh chilli (as per taste), chopped finely

2 teaspoons fresh ginger, grated

1teaspoon ground turmeric

1 teaspoon garam masala

1 teaspoon of ground cumin

2 cups of water

2 cups of basmati rice

¼ cup of lemon juice

1 litre of vegetable stock

Place dried chickpeas in a bowl of water, leave overnight. Drain and rinse. Place onions, garlic, chilli, ginger, tumeric, garam masala and curmin in a fry-pan and sauté until onions soften. Add chickpeas, rice, lemon juice and stock, bring to the boil, then reduce heat and simmer covered for 30 minutes, until chickpeas and rice are tender and liquid is absorbed. Simmer uncovered a further 10 minutes, if required, to cook off any extra fluid. Serve.

Total cooking time: 12 hours soaking, 50 minutes cooking
Serves: 4

Indian Style Red Lentil Pilau
Carbohydrate

This authentic Indian recipe gives you the choice of making your own garam masala or using the shop bought variety — personally I prefer the home-made variety.

2 tablespoons cumin seeds

1 tablespoon black peppercorns

2 teaspoons whole cloves

2 tablespoons coriander seeds

2 teaspoons cardamom seeds

1 cinnamon stick

½ teaspoon ground nutmeg

1 onion, finely chopped

3 cloves garlic, crushed

1 cup basmati rice

1 cup red lentils

3 cups hot vegetable stock

Seasoning

Spring onions, sliced to garnish

Fresh coriander leaves to garnish

Place all spices into a non-stick frypan and stir-fry for 1-2 minutes.
Remove from pan and grind to create a powdery texture. Return
3 teaspoons of mixed spices to frypan with onion, garlic and
2 tablespoons of water, stir-fry 3 minutes or until onion softens.
Add rice and lentils to the pan and stir-fry 3-5 minutes or until rice
grains begin to brown. Add the stock and bring to the boil, reduce
heat and simmer covered for 20 minutes or until rice is cooked and
stock is absorbed. Remove cover and stir-fry for a few minutes to cook
off excess fluid. Season as required and serve garnished with spring
onions and coriander.

Total cooking time: 40 minutes
Serves: 4

Spicy Roasted Vegetable Paella with Chickpeas

Carbohydrate

1 red Spanish onion, ends intact, cut into 8 wedges

1 large sweet potato, cut into 2cm cubes

4 baby yellow squash, halved

1 medium zucchini, sliced

2 medium tomatoes, cut into wedges

Salt and pepper to season

2 red capsicum, seeded and quartered

2 cloves garlic

1½ cups basmati rice

¼ – ½ red chilli, seeded and finely chopped

Pinch saffron threads

1 teaspoon black peppercorns

2 tablespoons tomato paste (no added sugar)

2 tablespoons lemon juice

3 cups vegetable stock

1 cup cooked chickpeas

½ cup fresh coriander leaves, chopped

Salt and pepper to taste

Extra coriander leaves to garnish

To a large baking tray, add onion, sweet potato, yellow squash, zucchini and tomatoes. Season and bake at 200°C for 50-60 minutes or until browned and cooked through.

Place capsicum under the grill, skin side up and grill until skin is blackened and blistered. Remove from grill and allow to cool before peeling.

Heat a large non-stick saucepan, add garlic, rice, chilli, saffron threads and black peppercorns. Stir-fry 3 minutes or until rice grains begin to brown. Add tomato paste, lemon juice and stock; mix well, bring to the boil, reduce heat and allow to simmer covered for 30 minutes or until rice is cooked. Add roasted vegetables, capsicum, chickpeas, coriander and seasoning. Mix well and heat through; cook off any excess fluid. Serve garnished with coriander

Total cooking time:1 hour
Serves: 4-6

Risotto with Fresh Dill and Roasted Tomato Wedges
Carbohydrate

3 medium tomatoes, cut into wedges

1 large onion, sliced

1 celery stick, sliced thinly

20 mushrooms, peeled, stalk removed and sliced

Salt and pepper

1½ cups basmati rice

6 cups vegetable stock

1 bunch fresh dill, chopped

½ lemon, juice

Salt and pepper to taste

Place tomato wedges in a non-stick baking tray. Roast 30 minutes at 200°C. Heat a large non-stick saucepan, add onion with 2 tablespoons of water and sauté until onion is soft and translucent. Add celery and mushrooms and 3 tablespoons of water and cook over medium heat for 5 minutes or until mushrooms begin to soften. Add rice and a dash of seasoning. Stir-fry 5 minutes over high heat or until grains begin to brown. Add 1 cup of vegetable stock, when all fluid has been absorbed add another cup of vegetable stock. Continue with the same process until all the vegetable stock has been used or the rice is soft and cooked through. Fold roasted tomato wedges, dill, lemon juice and any extra seasoning required, through the risotto. Heat through. Serve.

Total cooking time: 1 hour
Serves: 6

POULTRY

Chicken Cacciatore

Spicy Barbeque Chicken

Chicken and Proscuitto with Creamy Cheese Sauce

Chicken with Fennel and Feta Cheese

Hot Roast Chicken with Herbed Stuffing

Steamed Ginger Chicken with Asian Greens

Chicken, Parmesan and Spinach Loaf

Green Curry Chicken

Chicken and Mushrooms with Mustard Sauce

Chicken Cacciatore
Protein

3 chicken breast fillets, skins off, cut in half

4 tablespoons olive oil

1 large onion, sliced

2 cloves garlic, crushed

4 large tomatoes, diced

20 button mushrooms, sliced

2 tablespoons tomato paste (no added sugar)

2 cups hot water

2 bay leaves

¾ teaspoon allspice

¼ – ½ teaspoon cayenne pepper

Salt and pepper to taste

Heat oil in a large fry pan. Fry chicken over high heat 2 minutes each side, remove from pan and drain on paper towel. Add onion and garlic to the fry pan and cook 3 minutes or until onion has softened. Add mushrooms and tomatoes and heat through 5 minutes. Combine tomato paste, hot water, bay leaves, allspice, cayenne pepper and seasoning. Place chicken pieces in a large baking tray, spread tomato, mushroom and onion mixture on top and pour over liquid and spice mixture. Bake in oven 1 hour covered at 180°C, bake uncovered an extra 30 minutes or until sauce thickens.

Total cooking time:1 hour 30 minutes cooking, 20 minutes preparation
Serves: 4

Spicy Barbeque Chicken
Protein

1 small onion, chopped

3 tablespoons tomato paste (no added sugar)

2 teaspoons fresh ginger, grated

2 cloves garlic, crushed

1 teaspoon ground coriander

¼ teaspoon cayenne pepper

1 whole clove

1 teaspoon cumin seeds

1 teaspoon salt

1 teaspoon garam masala

4 breast chicken fillets, skin off

1 lemon, cut into wedges

Combine all ingredients (except chicken) in a food processor to form a paste. Baste chicken fillets in the paste, place in a sealed container and leave overnight in the refrigerator. Bake chicken uncovered at 200°C for 30 minutes. Turn over and coat with more marinade, bake a further 10-15 minutes. Serve with lemon wedges and Indian Style Vegetables.

Total cooking time: 24 hours marinating, 45 minutes cooking
Serves: 4

Chicken and Prosciutto with Creamy Cheese Sauce

Protein

4 tablespoons butter

2 cloves garlic, crushed

2 tablespoons fresh marjoram, finely chopped

2 tablespoons fresh sage leaves, finely chopped

1 tablespoon rosemary, finely chopped

1 teaspoon freshly cracked black pepper

4 chicken breast fillets, skin off

4 slices prosciutto

125g cream cheese, softened

2 tablespoons cream

1 egg yolk

Extra rosemary sprigs to garnish

Melt butter in a small saucepan. Add garlic, marjoram, sage, rosemary and black pepper and sauté briefly. Pound each chicken fillet out to 2-3 cm thickness. Brush with herb butter. Place one piece of prosciutto under each chicken fillet and roll up. Wrap each chicken and prosciutto roll in aluminum foil. Place in oven at 220°C for 25-30 minutes. Place cream and cheese in a small saucepan and warm gently until melted to form a smooth creamy sauce. Whisk egg yolk with 1 teaspoon of water and slowly add to cheese sauce, whisk thoroughly to combine. Unwrap chicken from foil and serve onto four plates, pour over cheese sauce and garnish with rosemary. You may wish to serve this dish with a suitable protein style side-dish or mixed lettuce tossed in a light vinaigrette of fresh parsley and roasted garlic

Total cooking time: 35 minutes
Serves: 4

Chicken with Fennel and Feta Cheese

Protein

2 tablespoons olive oil

3 chicken breast fillets, thinly sliced

1 red Spanish onion, sliced

2 cloves garlic, crushed

2 small fennel bulbs, sliced

2 teaspoons fresh thyme

¾ cup chicken or vegetable stock

½ cup cream

90g feta cheese, crumbled

Salt and pepper as per taste

4 cups mixed lettuce leaves

Heat olive oil in a large wok, stir-fry chicken until browned. Remove chicken from wok. Add onion and garlic to the wok, stir fry 3 minutes until onion softens. Add fennel and thyme and stir fry a further 5 minutes. Add chicken, stock and seasoning to the wok, bring to the boil, reduce heat and simmer 10 minutes or until fluid has condensed. Add cream and cheese and gently heat through. Serve with lettuce or suitable protein side-dish.

Total cooking time: 30 minutes
Serves: 4

Hot Roast Chicken with Herbed Stuffing

Protein

1 medium size whole chicken

1 large zucchini, grated and squeezed of excess fluid

1 large white onion, finely chopped

3 rashers of bacon, chopped

1 tablespoon of butter

1 cup fresh parsley, finely chopped

1 tablespoon fresh rosemary, chopped

1 tablespoon lemon juice

1 teaspoon salt

¼ teaspoon black pepper

¼ cup vegetable oil

2 tablespoons salt, extra

2 tablespoons mixed dried herbs

lemon zest, grated

Add onion bacon and butter to a frypan, stir-fry for 3 minutes.
Add zucchini and continue to stir-fry 5 minutes or until fluid has
condensed. Combine zucchini and onion with parsley, rosemary, lemon
juice, salt and pepper. Stuff chicken with zucchini mixture and close
with skewers. Cover chicken in vegetable oil, rub in salt and lemon
zest, sprinkle over dried herbs. Place chicken on a greased baking tray
in the oven at 180°C for 60 minutes. Serve chicken with stuffing and
steamed or roasted zucchini, baby yellow squash and cauliflower.
Use Hollandaise sauce as a gravy substitute.

Total cooking time: 20 minutes preparation, 60 minutes cooking
Serves: 4-6

Steamed Ginger Chicken with Asian Greens
Protein

A large bamboo steamer works best for this dish, however you can use a metal steamer if necessary.

1 tablespoon fresh ginger grated

1 tablespoon lemon juice

2 teaspoons sesame oil

Salt and pepper to taste

8 chicken thigh fillets, skin off, sliced

1 cup dried, sliced Chinese mushrooms

4 spring onions sliced, trimmed and sliced

1 tablespoon extra ginger, chopped

4 choy sum (Chinese broccoli), trimmed and chopped

1 teaspoon sesame oil, extra

2 tablespoons peanut oil

4 bok choy, ends removed

Combine ginger, lemon juice, sesame oil and seasoning in a mixing bowl. Add sliced chicken and coat well with marinade. Cover and place in refrigerator and marinate for at least 2 hours.

To a bowl add 2 cups of boiling water and mushrooms, leave to soak 20 minutes before draining and setting aside.

Place marinated chicken into a large bamboo steamer, place onion, mushrooms and extra ginger on top. Steam covered 20-25 minutes, or until chicken is cooked through.

In a small saucepan heat left over marinade, bring to the boil, reduce heat and allow to simmer slowly until reduced to 4 tablespoons of fluid.

Steam choy sum briefly. Then add to wok with extra sesame oil and peanut oil, stir-fry 1 minute.

Serve steamed chicken with onion and mushrooms onto plates with the stir-fried Asian greens. Drizzle over one tablespoon of the reduced marinade fluid. Serve immediately.

Total cooking time: 2 hours marinating, 30 minutes cooking
Serves: 4

Chicken, Parmesan and Spinach Loaf

Protein

2 chicken breast fillets, skin off

1 tablespoon olive oil

1 white onion, finely chopped

2 rashers bacon, diced

250g cooked spinach, well drained and squeezed

¾ cup olive oil, extra

2 cloves garlic, crushed

2 eggs

2 egg yolks

1 teaspoon mustard powder

¾ cup grated parmesan cheese

½ cup sour cream

4 tablespoons fresh parsley, finely chopped

Salt and pepper to taste

220g grated tasty cheese

1 teaspoon paprika

Poach chicken and shred. Fry onion and bacon in 1 tablespoon olive oil. Combine shredded chicken, onion, bacon, and spinach and mix well. Spoon into the bottom of a baking dish. Combine extra olive oil, garlic, eggs, egg yolks, mustard, parmesan cheese, sour cream, parsley and seasoning in a blender. Pour over chicken and spinach mixture. Top with grated cheese and sprinkle with paprika. Bake uncovered in oven 35 minutes at 180°C or until browned. Serve with an appropriate protein side-dish.

Total cooking time: 50 minutes
Serves: 4

Green Curry Chicken

Protein

4 chicken breast fillets, skin off

4 tablespoons green curry paste

2 tablespoons oil

1 large onion, sliced

4 tablespoons sour cream

½ cup fresh coriander leaves, chopped

Rub green curry paste into chicken fillets. Heat oil in a large frypan, add chicken and onion and fry until chicken is cooked through. Add sour cream and coriander and gently heat. Serve garnished with extra coriander alongside mixed lettuce drizzled with Light Vinaigrette.

Total cooking time: 40 minutes
Serves: 4

Chicken and Mushrooms with Mustard Sauce

Protein

4 tablespoons olive oil

4 breast chicken fillets, skin off, cut into strips

¾ teaspoon ground turmeric

½ teaspoon ground cumin

Salt and pepper to taste

20 button mushrooms, quartered

10 pink peppercorns

1 teaspoon lemon juice

1 tablespoon olive oil, extra

2 teaspoons mustard (no added sugar)

½ cup cream

3 tablespoons grated parmesan cheese

3 tablespoons grated tasty cheese

3 cups mixed lettuce leaves

Heat olive oil in a large wok, add chicken and stir-fry, add turmeric, and seasoning and continue to stir-fry until chicken is golden brown; remove from wok. Add mushrooms to the wok and stir-fry until soft and well cooked, add peppercorns, chicken and lemon juice. Stir-fry a further minute.

Gently heat cream, mustard and cheeses until all cheese is melted. Divide lettuce between four plates, top with chicken and mushroom mixture and pour over sauce.

Total cooking time: 25 minutes
Serves: 4

MEAT

Asian Style Spicy Mince in Lettuce Cups

Mediterranean Lamb Stir-Fry

Lamb Masaman Curry Casserole

Meat Loaf with Blue Cheese Sauce

Schnitzel

Kangaroo with Leeks and Lemon Dressing

Easy Beef Stroganoff

Stuffed Lamb Fillets with Grilled Vegetables and Pesto

Curried Veal and Vegetables

Lamb and Artichoke Kebabs

Cordon Bleu Meat Balls

Roast Lamb and Vegetables with Cheese Sauce and Pesto

Spicy Mince Burgers with Salsa

Asian Style Spicy Mince in Lettuce Cups
Protein

1 teaspoon sesame oil

2 tablespoons peanut oil

1 clove garlic

1 teaspoon fresh ginger, grated

500g mince meat of choice

225g can sliced bamboo shoots, drained

4 medium tomatoes, diced

1 lime, juice

1-2 teaspoons Tabasco sauce, as per taste

2 cups bean shoots

¾ cup fresh coriander leaves, chopped

Salt and pepper to taste

1 large lettuce, halved, outer leaves removed

Heat oil in large wok, add garlic and ginger. Stir-fry 1 minute.
Add meat and stir-fry over high heat for 5 minutes or until browned.
Add bamboo shoots, tomatoes, lime juice and Tabasco sauce. Mix well
and stir fry 5 minutes until heated through. Add bean shoots,
coriander and seasoning and stir-fry a further 5 minutes or until
excess fluid has been cooked off. Serve meat mixture in lettuce cups.

Total cooking time: 20 minutes
Serves: 4

Mediterranean Lamb Stir-Fry
Protein

3 red capsicum, seeded and quartered

2 tablespoons olive oil

3 baby eggplants, peeled and sliced

1 fennel bulb, sliced

410g lamb backstrap, thinly sliced

2 cloves garlic, crushed

1 tablespoon fresh oregano, chopped

Dash Tabasco

Salt and pepper

1 tablespoon plain white vinegar

6 slices of prosciutto, roughly chopped

½ cup fresh flat leaf parley, chopped

Place capsicum under a grill, skin side up. Grill until skin blackens and blisters. Remove from grill, allow to cool before peeling. Heat oil in a large wok, add eggplant and fennel. Stir-fry 5 minutes or until browned and cooked through. Remove from wok and set aside. Add lamb in batches to the wok with garlic, oregano, Tabasco sauce and seasoning. Stir-fry lamb until browned and cooked through. Add capsicum, fennel, eggplant, vinegar, prosciutto and parsley to the wok and stir-fry a further 2-3 minutes. Serve.

Total cooking time: 35 minutes
Serves: 4

Lamb Masaman Curry Casserole

Protein

2 tablespoons olive oil

1 large onion sliced

2 medium zucchini, cut into 2.5cm slices

4 tomatoes, diced

½ head broccoli, break into florets

½ head cauliflower, break into florets

4 baby yellow squash, quartered

500g diced lamb or beef

2 tablespoons tomato paste

4 cups hot vegetable stock

2 tablespoons masaman curry paste

Salt to taste

Serve garnished with a dollop of sour cream and fresh coriander.

Heat olive oil in a saucepan, add onion and sauté 3 minutes or until onion is soft. To a large casserole dish add onion, zucchini, tomatoes, broccoli, cauliflower, yellow squash and lamb. In a mixing bowl, combine tomato paste, vegetable stock, masaman curry paste and seasoning. Pour over meat and vegetables. Place casserole in oven covered, at 150°C for 2 hours. Uncover and bake a further 30 minutes or until fluid has cooked off to make a thick sauce. Serve in large serving bowls and garnish with a dollop of sour cream and fresh coriander.

Total cooking time: 2 hours 45 minutes
Serves: 6

Meat Loaf with Blue Cheese Sauce

Protein

1 tablespoon butter

1 large onion, finely chopped

500g mince meat

1 medium zucchini, grated and squeezed of excess fluid

3 tablespoons tomato paste (no added sugar)

2 eggs, lightly beaten

1 tablespoon mixed dried herbs

Seasoning

1 tablespoon butter

1 clove garlic, crushed

60g crumbled blue cheese

1½ tablespoons cream

Parsley to garnish

Stir-fry onion with butter until onion softens. Add zucchini and stir-fry a further 8 minutes or until fluid is mostly evaporated. Combine mince, zucchini, onion, tomato paste, eggs, mixed herbs and seasoning, place in greased loaf tin, cover and bake at 200°C for 1 hour.

Heat oil in a saucepan, sauté garlic. Add cheese and cream and heat on very low gas until cheese has melted.

Turn out meat loaf, slice. Place slices on plates and pour over blue cheese sauce. Garnish with parsley. Serve this dish with steamed baby yellow squash and zucchini .

Total cooking time: 1 hour cooking, 15 minutes preparation
Serves: 4

Schnitzel

Protein

2 medium eggplants, peeled and diced into 1cm pieces

3 teaspoons salt

3 medium tomatoes

2 tablespoons olive oil

1 medium onion, finely chopped

2 cloves garlic, crushed

1 tablespoon tomato paste (no added sugar)

¼ cup fresh basil, finely chopped

Salt and pepper to taste

4 beef or veal schnitzel steaks, tenderized

1 cup grated Mozzarella cheese

1 cup grated tasty cheese

½ cup shaved parmesan cheese

Extra shaved parmesan to garnish

Parsley to garnish

Sprinkle diced eggplant with salt. Place in a colander with a weighted plate on top. Stand in the sink for two hours to allow the fluid to drain away. After two hours, rinse eggplant and pat dry.

Mark a cross in the bottom of each tomato. Drop tomatoes one at a time, into boiling water for 30 seconds. Remove skin and dice.

Heat oil in a large saucepan, add onion and garlic and stir-fry until onion softens. Add eggplant, tomato, tomato paste, basil and seasoning. Cook 5 minutes over medium heat to make a thick sauce-like consistency. Grill meat 1 minute each side on a very hot griddle plate. Divide meat amongst four plates, spoon over tomato and eggplant mixture and top with cheeses. Place each plate under a grill until cheese is melted and browned. Serve garnished with parsley and extra parmesan cheese shavings.

Total cooking time: 2 hours standing, 15 minutes preparation,
35 minutes cooking
Serves: 4

Kangaroo with Leeks and Lemon Dressing
Protein

Kangaroo is my favourite meat. It is lean, fresh tasting, free of antibiotics and hormones, and it's very Australian. When cooked correctly, kangaroo meat should be very tender, like the best steak you have ever had. If you have never tried kangaroo, well here's your chance. I am not sure of the availability of kangaroo meat outside of Australia, but I am sure this wonderful meat will eventually become readily available internationally.

4 × 220g kangaroo sirloin

12 lemon myrtle leaves

8 slices of prosciutto

2 tablespoons vegetable oil

4 leeks, trimmed and cut into 6cm lengths

2 cups chicken stock

4 spring onions, minced

2 cloves garlic, crushed

3 tablespoons vegetable oil, extra

2 lemons juiced

1 lemon rind grated

Salt and pepper to season

Beat out sirloins to 1.5 cm thickness. Lay four lemon myrtle leaves on each sirloin. Roll up each sirloin with 2 slices of prosciutto, secure with a toothpick or string. Heat oil in a large fry pan. Add kangaroo rolls to the pan and cook briefly over high heat to seal the kangaroo meat. Place kangaroo rolls on a greased oven tray and bake at 180°C for 10-15 minutes.

Bring chicken stock to the boil, add leeks, reduce heat and simmer for 20 minutes. Drain leeks, reserving 3 tablespoons of stock.

Heat extra oil in a small saucepan. Add spring onions and garlic and sauté briefly until onion begins to soften. Remove from heat and add reserved chicken stock, lemon juice, lemon zest and seasoning. Mix well. Arrange kangaroo and leeks between four plates and pour over lemon and spring onion dressing. Serve.

Total cooking time: 30 minutes
Serves: 4

Easy Beef Stroganoff
Protein

500g blade steak, diced

2 large onions, sliced

2 cloves garlic, crushed

250g mushrooms, peeled and sliced

6 large tomatoes, diced

1 tablespoon tomato paste

¾ cup vegetable stock

¼ cup fresh parsley, finely chopped

Salt and pepper to season.

4 tablespoons sour cream

To a large casserole dish add steak, onions, garlic, mushrooms, tomatoes, tomato paste, stock, parsley and seasoning. Combine well, cover and bake in oven at 200°C for 1 hour. Uncover and bake a further 20 minutes. Stir through sour cream and heat gently over low gas. Serve with appropriate protein side-dish such as blanched green vegetables with parsley and garlic vinaigrette.

Total cooking time: 15 minutes preparation, 1 hour 20 minutes cooking
Serves: 4

Stuffed Lamb Fillets with Grilled Vegetables and Pesto

Protein

4 lamb backstraps

3 bocconcini, sliced

60g semi sun-dried tomatoes

2 tablespoons fresh basil leaves

3 medium zucchinis, sliced lengthways

2 medium eggplants, sliced

3 baby yellow squash, sliced

¼ cup olive oil

2 cloves garlic crushed

1 tablespoon mixed dried herbs

4 tablespoons pesto

Flatten out individual backstraps. Layer with cheese, tomato and basil. Roll up and tie each firmly with string. Prepare vegetables. Combine olive oil, garlic, herbs and seasoning. Brush backstrap and vegetables with olive oil. Cook backstraps and vegetables on a griddle plate until well browned and cooked through. Serve on four plates and top with pesto.

Total cooking time: 30 minutes
Serves: 4

Curried Veal and Vegetables
Protein

625g veal topside

2 teaspoons curry powder

1 teaspoon cumin

1 teaspoon coriander powder

1 teaspoon paprika

1 teaspoon salt

1 teaspoon powdered black pepper

2 tablespoons olive oil

3 yellow capsicum, seeded and quartered

8 yellow squash, quartered

2 yellow zucchinis, quartered

1 stick lemongrass, finely chopped

1 teaspoon fresh ginger, grated

1 clove garlic, crushed

¾ teaspoon of ground turmeric powder

1 red chilli, seeded and finely chopped

1 tablespoon musaman curry paste

Salt and pepper to season

¾ cup of chicken or vegetable stock

2 tomatoes, diced

¾ cup sour cream

½ cup fresh coriander leaves, chopped

Fresh coriander to garnish

Roll veal in curry powder, cumin, coriander powder, paprika, salt and pepper. Heat olive oil in a large saucepan add meat and sear all sides. Place meat on greased baking tray and cook uncovered at 180°C for 30 minutes. Set aside for 10 minutes before slicing to serve.

Place capsicum under a hot grill, skin side up until skin blackens and blisters, allow capsicum to cool before peeling.

To the large saucepan, add the squash and zucchini; stir-fry 5 minutes over high heat until lightly browned. To vegetables, add lemongrass, ginger, garlic, turmeric, curry paste, chilli and seasoning; stir-fry 1 minute. Add stock and tomatoes, simmer uncovered for 20 minutes. Stir through sour cream, coriander and capsicum and heat through.

Divide veal between four plates. Serve with curried vegetables and garnish with fresh coriander.

Total cooking time: 40 minutes
Serves: 4

Lamb and Artichoke Kebabs

Protein

500g diced lamb

410g can artichoke hearts, drained and halved

1 large red capsicum, seeded and chopped

315g button mushrooms, halved

1 cup olive oil

4 cloves garlic, crushed

½ cup fresh basil leaves, chopped

2 tablespoons fresh marjoram, chopped

1 tablespoon fresh thyme leaves, chopped

1 teaspoon mustard powder

Soak bamboo skewers in water for 1 hour to prevent them scorching.
Thread lamb, artichoke hearts, capsicum and mushrooms onto skewers.
Place in a large dish. Combine other ingredients, pour over kebabs.
Cover and marinate overnight. Grill or barbeque kebabs.

Total cooking time: 15 minutes preparation, 12 hours marinating,
15 minutes cooking
Makes: 12 kebabs

Cordon Bleu Meatballs

Protein

750g minced meat

1 large onion, finely chopped

3 egg whites, lightly beaten

2 tablespoons tomato paste (no added sugar)

1 teaspoon salt

½ teaspoon pepper

60g soft blue cheese

½ cup diced ham

Combine mince, onion, egg, tomato paste, salt and pepper. Wrap mince around small pieces of blue cheese and ham to form meat balls. Place on greased baking tray and bake 30 minutes at 180°C or until browned and cooked through. To serve, pour over Hollandaise sauce and serve with broccoli and cauliflower alfredo.

Total cooking time: 15 minutes preparation, 30 minutes cooking
Makes: 16 meatballs

Roast Lamb and Vegetables with Creamy Cheese Sauce and Pesto

Protein

1kg butterflied boned lamb shoulder

90g butter, softened

1 tablespoon grated lemon rind

2 tablespoons fresh parsley, finely chopped

2 teaspoons, fresh thyme, finely chopped

2 cloves garlic, crushed

Salt and pepper to season

2 tablespoons olive oil

3 small red Spanish onions, quartered

3 medium zucchini, chunked

3 baby eggplants, peeled and chunked

1 red capsicum, seeded and quartered

1 green capsicum, seeded and quartered

4 baby yellow squash, quartered

4 tablespoons cream

2 tablespoons grated parmesan cheese

4 tablespoons pesto

Open lamb out flat, with fat side down. Pound with a mallet to even thickness. Combine butter, rind, parsley, thyme, garlic and seasoning, rub into meat. Heat oil in a large baking dish. Cook lamb over high gas, uncovered until browned both sides; remove from dish. Add vegetables to the baking dish and stir-fry until lightly browned. Place lamb fat side up on top of vegies. Cook uncovered, in the oven at 200°C for 30 minutes. Remove lamb from oven and cover with aluminium foil to keep warm. Return vegetables to the oven, bake uncovered at 200°C for 15 minutes or until well browned and cooked through. Set vegetables aside, drain and reserve pan juices.

To a small saucepan add reserved pan juices, cream and parmesan cheese. Warm sauce over very low heat until all cheese has melted. Slice lamb into 2.5 cm slices. Divide vegetables and lamb between six plates. Drizzle sauce over top and then pesto.

Total cooking time: 1 hour
Serves: 6

Spicy Mince Burgers with Salsa
Protein

500g mince meat

2 tablespoons tomato paste (no added sugar)

2 teaspoons curry powder

1 teaspoon chilli flakes

2 egg whites, lightly beaten

Salsa

Combine meat, tomato paste, curry powder, chilli flakes and egg whites; mix together well. Divide meat into burger size patties. Heat a fry pan with a little oil. Add burgers a few at a time, cooking 4 minutes each side or until browned and cooked through. Serve burgers with salsa and suitable protein style side-dish or mixed lettuce leaves with suitable protein style dressing.

Total cooking time: 10 minutes preparation, 15 minutes cooking
Makes: 12 burgers

SEAFOOD

Greek Style Fish

Salmon, Dill and Marscapone Muffins with Mayonnaise

Curried Octopus with Tomatoes and Tamarind

Roasted Ocean Trout with Wasabi Dressing and Nori

Fresh Prawn Curry with Lemon Myrtle

Spicy Fish Cakes with Vietnamese Style Dressing

Fish and Red Capsicum Terrine

Cajun Seafood with Vegetables

Garlic Prawns with Creamy Cheese Sauce

Vietnamese Style Barramundi

Fried Whitebait with Lemon and Mustard Dressing

Salmon with Leeks and Oyster Mushrooms

Greek Style Fish
Protein

60g haloumi cheese, diced

¼ cup olive oil

2 cloves garlic, crushed

1 tablespoon mixed dried herbs

2 tablespoons olive oil, extra

6 Roma tomatoes, halved

2 red Spanish onions, ends intact, cut into wedges

3 red capsicum, seeded and quartered

2 tablespoons olive oil

1 leek, trimmed and sliced

2 cloves garlic

1 teaspoon black peppercorns

1 tablespoon lemon juice

1kg boneless white fish fillets, chopped

2 tablespoons fresh basil, chopped

1 tablespoon fresh oregano, chopped

1 tablespoon fresh marjoram, chopped

1 teaspoon lemon zest

1 tablespoon vinegar

Salt and pepper to taste

Combine haloumi, olive oil, garlic and mixed herbs. Allow to marinate for two hours then grill haloumi under a hot grill until browned both sides. Reserve 4 tablespoons of marinade.

Add 2 tablespoons of extra olive oil to a baking tray. Add tomatoes and onions. Place in the oven at 180°C for 1 hour.

Place capsicum under a hot grill, skin side up. Grill until skin becomes blackened and blistered. Remove and allow to cool.
Peel and discard skin.

To a large wok add 2 tablespoons of haloumi marinade, leek, garlic and peppercorns, sauté 2 minutes. Add lemon juice and fish and stir-fry 2 minutes. Add haloumi, tomato, onion, capsicum, basil, oregano, marjoram, lemon zest, vinegar, 2 tablespoons of olive oil from haloumi marinade and seasoning. Toss briefly over high heat.
Serve on 4 plates.

Total cooking time: 2 hours marinating, 30 minutes cooking
Serves: 4

Salmon, Dill and Mascarpone Muffins with Creamy Lemon Mayonnaise

Protein

2 tablespoons olive oil

½ green capsicum, seeded and chopped finely

½ red capsicum, seeded and chopped finely

8 spring onions, trimmed and sliced

220g can of salmon, drained and bones removed

4 tablespoons fresh dill, finely chopped

4 tablespoons fresh mascarpone cheese, softened

2 eggs, beaten

Salt and cracked black peppercorns to season

½ cup creamy lemon mayonnaise

Heat oil in a saucepan, add capsicum and onion. Sauté 5 minutes or until softened. In a blender combine salmon, dill, mascarpone, eggs and seasoning until well blended. Fold through capsicum and onion. Grease a muffin tray and divide mixture between muffin wells. Place in oven at 180°C for 20-25 minutes or until browned and egg has set. Turn out muffins onto plates and drizzle mayonnaise over top. Serve with suitable protein style side-dish such as broccoli and cauliflower alfredo, or by itself as an entrée.

Total cooking time: 20 minutes preparation, 25 minutes cooking
Makes: 6 large muffins

Curried Octopus with Tomatoes and Tamarind

Protein

2 tablespoons ghee or butter

1 onion, sliced

2 cloves garlic, crushed

2 teaspoons fresh ginger, grated

1 stick cinnamon

2 teaspoons ground cumin

½ teaspoon ground turmeric

¼ teaspoon chilli powder

2 teaspoons ground coriander

1 teaspoon tamarind puree

4 tomatoes, peeled and diced

1 tablespoon tomato paste

¼ cup chicken stock

1kg baby octopus

4 tablespoons sour cream

Heat ghee in a large saucepan; add onion, garlic and ginger and stir-fry 2 minutes. Add cinnamon, cumin, turmeric and chilli and stir-fry 1 minute. Add tamarind puree, tomatoes, tomato paste and stock; bring to the boil; reduce heat and simmer 15 minutes uncovered. Prepare octopus by discarding heads and beaks and cutting the tentacles into quarters. Add octopus to tomato and tamarind mixture, cover and simmer 3 minutes. Add sour cream and heat through.

Total cooking time: 20 minutes
Serves: 4

Roasted Ocean Trout with Wasabi Dressing and Nori Crisps

Protein

2 sheets nori

2 teaspoons of sesame oil, extra

Dash of pepper

4 ocean trout fillets

2 teaspoons sesame oil

Salt

¾ cup sour cream

1 teaspoon wasabi paste

1 teaspoon fresh ginger, minced

½ lime juice

315g English spinach leaves, trimmed and washed

Brush nori with a little sesame oil and season with black pepper. Cut into thin strips then place on a baking tray and bake for 10 minutes at 200°C then set aside.

Place fish on a greased baking tray. Brush with sesame oil and sprinkle with a little salt. Bake at 100°C for 25-30 minutes.

Combine sour cream, wasabi, ginger and lime juice, set aside.

Steam spinach briefly, drain and divide between four plates. Serve trout on top of spinach, garnish with a dollop of wasabi dressing and nori crisps.

Total cooking time: 40 minutes
Serves: 4

Fresh Prawn Curry with Lemon Myrtle

Protein

100 ml fish or chicken stock

4 fresh or dried lemon myrtle leaves

4 tablespoons peanut oil

1 teaspoon sesame oil

1 onion, finely chopped

1 clove garlic, crushed

2 teaspoons fresh ginger, finely chopped

1 tablespoon red curry paste

32 large green king prawns, peeled and deveined

4 tablespoons fish sauce

Seasoning

3 tablespoons sour cream

4 tablespoons fresh basil leaves, chopped

1 bunch fresh coriander leaves, chopped

4 spring onions, sliced

Heat stock, add lemon myrtle leaves and stand 20 minutes. Heat oils in a large wok. Add onion, garlic and ginger and stir-fry 2 minutes. Add red curry paste and stir-fry 1 minute. Add prawns, stir-fry 1 minute. Add fish sauce, seasoning, stock and lemon myrtle leaves to the wok, bring to the boil, then reduce heat. Add sour cream, coriander, basil and spring onions. Heat through gently. Serve with suitable protein style side-dish such as Indian style vegetables.

Total cooking time: 25 minutes
Serves: 4

Spicy Fish Cakes with Vietnamese Style Dressing
Protein

1 cucumber, finely chopped

1 red chilli, seeded and finely chopped

½ cup fresh coriander leaves, chopped

500g prawns, peeled, deveined and chopped

250g white fish, skinned, boned and chopped

1 tablespoon green curry paste

1 lime, juice

2 tablespoons water

Salt and pepper to season

2 tablespoons peanut oil

2 red chillies (extra), seeded and finely chopped

6 cloves garlic, crushed

2 tablespoons fresh ginger, grated

1 teaspoon coarse salt

4 tablespoons fish sauce

4 tablespoons lime juice

2 tablespoons water, extra

Combine cucumber, chilli, coriander, prawns, fish, curry paste, lime juice, water and seasoning and process in a blender to form a smooth paste. Form into 32 small flat patties and fry with peanut oil until golden brown. Place extra chillies, garlic, ginger and salt in a mortar, grind into a paste, add fish sauce, lime and extra water, mix well. Serve fish cakes with dressing drizzled over top.

Total cooking time: 20 minutes
Makes: 32 patties

Fish and Red Capsicum Terrine

Protein

4 red capsicums, seeded and quartered

500g white fish fillets, skin and bones removed

1 cup sour cream

½ cup fresh basil, chopped

2 tablespoons fresh chives, chopped

2 teaspoons gelatine

¼ cup boiling hot water

Salt and pepper to taste

Place capsicum under a hot grill, skin up. Grill until skin blackens and blisters. Remove and place in a plastic bag to cool. When cooled, remove skin.

Poach fish, then process fish and cream together to form a smooth consistency. Fold through basil, chives and seasoning.

Combine gelatin and water. Whisk and allow to cool slightly, then add to fish mixture; mix well. Place half the fish mixture in the bottom of a well oiled loaf tin. Layer capsicum on top, then add the remaining fish mixture. Refrigerate covered for 12 hours. Turn out and slice into 2.5 cm slices. Serve with creamy lemon mayonnaise.

Total cooking time: 20 minutes preparation, 12 hours refrigeration
Serves: 6

Cajun Seafood with Vegetables
Protein

2 cloves garlic, crushed

1 tablespoon Cajun seasoning

1 tablespoon olive oil

1 kg white fish fillets, skin and boned removed

1 tablespoon olive oil, extra

1 large onion, sliced

1 green pepper, seeded and sliced

4 yellow squash, quartered

2 small zucchinis, chunked

4 tomatoes, diced

½ cup fish stock

½ teaspoon Tabasco sauce

4 tablespoons fresh basil, chopped

155g fresh baby prawns, peeled

Combine garlic, Cajun seasoning and oil to form a paste. Roughly chop fish fillets and coat with paste, refrigerate at least 2 hours. Heat extra oil in a large fry pan, add onion, pepper, squash and zucchini, stir-fry 5 minutes. Add tomatoes, stock, Tabasco and basil, bring to boil, reduce heat and simmer 15 minutes. Add prawns and fish and simmer 5 minutes or until cooked through. Serve.

Total cooking time: 2 hours refrigeration, 30 minutes cooking
Serves: 4

Garlic Prawns with Creamy Cheese Sauce

Protein

4 tablespoons butter

1 kg green King prawns, peeled, deveined

4 cloves garlic, crushed

2 tablespoons cream

½ cup grated cheddar cheese

2 tablespoons parmesan cheese

1 tablespoon fresh chives, snipped

Heat butter in a large wok, add prawns and garlic and stir-fry until prawns are just tender and changing colour. Warm cheeses and cream over gentle heat to form a smooth sauce. Serve prawns onto plates and pour over melted cheese sauce. Garnish with chives.

Total cooking time: 20 minutes
Serves: 4

Vietnamese Style Barramundi
Protein

Barramundi is a wonderful fish found in the estuarine waters of northern Australia.

2 tablespoons fresh coriander, finely chopped

1 red chilli, finely chopped

1 green chilli, finely chopped

1 lemongrass stick, sliced

4 large barramundi cutlets

2 tablespoons peanut oil

90g shiitake mushrooms

½ head of broccoli florets

2 small zucchini, sliced lengthways

1-2 teaspoon red curry paste, as per taste

½ cup fish stock

Combine coriander, chillies and lemongrass in a mortar and grind into a paste. Cover fish with paste and refrigerate 10 minutes. Heat 1 tablespoon peanut oil in a large frypan, add fish and fry 3 minutes each side or until tender. Heat 1 tablespoon peanut oil in a large wok, add mushrooms, broccoli and zucchini and stir-fry 5 minutes. Add curry paste and fish stock, simmer until sauce reduces a little then serve with fish.

Total cooking time: 30 minutes
Serves: 4

Fried Whitebait with Lemon and Mustard Dressing

Protein

4 cups whitebait

Salt and pepper to season

Olive oil to shallow fry

2 egg yolks

1 teaspoon mustard powder

1 tablespoon sour cream

2 tablespoons lemon juice

2 cloves garlic, crushed

¾ cup olive oil

1 lemon, cut into wedges

Season white bait liberally, shallow fry in hot oil until browned and crisp, drain on a paper towel. Combine egg yolks, mustard, sour cream, lemon and garlic in a processor, slowly pour in the oil a little at a time until well combined. Serve whitebait on plates, pour dressing over top and garnish with lemon wedges. Serve with mixed lettuce.

Total cooking time: 15 minutes
Serves: 4

Salmon with Leeks and Oyster Mushrooms

Protein

2 tablespoons butter

1 leek, sliced

6 oyster mushrooms

3 tablespoons cream

Seasoning

2 teaspoons snipped chives

1 tablespoon oil

4 salmon steaks

Add butter, leek and mushrooms to a frypan and stir-fry until leek softens. Add cream, seasoning and chives, heat through.

Season salmon and cook in a frypan with 1 tablespoon of oil for 2 minutes each side. Serve salmon with leek and oyster mushroom sauce.

Total cooking time: 15 minutes
Serves: 4

EGGS AND CHEESE

Easy Bacon and Cheese Omelette

Warm Asparagus and Egg Salad with Hollandaise Sauce

Salsa Cheesecake

Egg and Zucchini Hash Browns

Spicy Egg Roll-Ups

Salsa Cheesecake

Baked Spinach Flan

Frittata

Easy Bacon and Cheese Omelette
Protein

2 tablespoons olive oil

4 rashers rindless bacon, chopped

20 mushrooms, peeled and sliced

9 eggs

220g grated tasty cheese

½ cup grated parmesan cheese

¾ cup cream

½ cup fresh parsley, finely chopped

¾ teaspoon ground nutmeg

Salt and pepper to taste

Heat olive oil in a saucepan, add bacon and mushrooms and fry 5 minutes or until well browned. Combine bacon and mushrooms and all other ingredients in a large square casserole dish. Mix well. Place in oven at 180°C for 45 minutes or until egg is set and omelette is well browned.

Total cooking time: 55 minutes
Serves: 6

Warm Asparagus and Egg Salad with Hollandaise Sauce

Protein

8 eggs

16 spears asparagus, trimmed

Shaved parmesan to garnish

½ cup Hollandaise sauce

Boil eggs 6-7 minutes, stirring occasionally to centre the yolks. Peel and halve lengthways. Cook asparagus 3 minutes in boiling water. Arrange asparagus and boiled eggs onto four plates. Pour over Hollandaise sauce and garnish with parmesan shavings.

Total cooking time: 15 minutes
Serves: 4

Salsa Cheesecake
Protein

250g cream cheese, softened

3 eggs, lightly beaten

½ cup salsa

½ cup sour cream

1 red capsicum, seeded and quartered

1 green capsicum, seeded and quartered

2 spring onions, sliced

½ cup grated tasty cheese

Combine cream cheese, eggs and salsa. Pour into a greased springform baking tin and bake 45 minutes at 180°C. Allow to cool 10 minutes, remove from tin and place in the refrigerator to chill. Place capsicum under a hot grill, skin side up. Grill until skin blackens and blisters. Remove from grill and place in a plastic bag and allow to cool. Once cooled, remove skin. Spread sour cream over baked salsa cheesecake, top with grilled capsicum, spring onions and grated cheese. Slice into wedges and serve.

Total cooking time: 1 hour cooking and preparation, 1 hour refrigeration
Serves: 4

Egg and Zucchini Hash Browns
Protein

8 eggs, lightly beaten

1 large zucchini, grated

4 tablespoons cream cheese, softened

¾ teaspoon nutmeg

Salt and pepper to season

1 tablespoon olive oil

Combine, eggs, zucchini, cream cheese, nutmeg and seasoning. Heat oil in a large fry pan. Pour egg mixture into egg-circles and cook until golden brown and egg is set. Serve with suitable protein-style dressing and side-dish.

Total cooking time: 30 minutes
Makes: 12 hash browns

Spicy Egg Roll-Ups

Protein

4 eggs

1 teaspoon fish sauce (no added sugar)

½ teaspoon salt

1 tablespoon fresh chives, chopped

2 tablespoons olive oil

1 teaspoon fresh ginger, minced

1 teaspoon garlic, crushed

1 teaspoon red chilli, chopped finely

½ tablespoon lemongrass, sliced

1 tablespoon fish sauce, extra (no added sugar)

125ml tomato juice (no added sugar)

1 tablespoon fresh coriander, chopped

155g packet cured sliced salmon, chopped

90g cucumber, finely diced

1 tablespoon fresh chives, chopped, extra

1 teaspoon fresh mint, chopped

Fresh chives to garnish

Combine eggs, fish sauce, salt and chives, beat well. Pour into a hot oiled fry pan a quarter of the egg mixture at a time to make 4 crepes. Cook to a very light brown colour, set aside.

In a small saucepan heat 2 tablespoons of olive oil, add ginger, garlic, chilli and lemongrass and stir-fry 2 minutes. Add extra fish sauce, tomato juice and coriander and heat through. Set sauce aside.

Combine salmon, cucumber, chives, mint and 3 tablespoons of prepared sauce; allow to stand 1 hour. Divide salmon mixture into four and place on crepes; roll up tightly. Cover with cling wrap and refrigerate 30 minutes. After refrigeration, slice each roll into three equal portions, arrange 3 portions on each of four plates and drizzle over prepared sauce. Garnish with fresh chives.

Total cooking time: 20 minutes cooking, 30 minutes refrigeration
Serves: 4

Baked Spinach Flan
Protein

This dish is great for taking to work to reheat for lunch.

2 large eggplants, peeled and sliced

1 tablespoon olive oil

1 large onion, chopped

2 cloves garlic, crushed

6 tomatoes, diced

3 tablespoons tomato paste

1 tablespoon fresh oregano, chopped

2 × 220g cans spinach, drained and squeezed of
   excess fluid

250g ricotta cheese

220g feta cheese

½ cup grated parmesan cheese

1 teaspoon ground nutmeg

¾ cup fresh basil, finely chopped

8 eggs, beaten

½ cup cream

220g grated tasty cheese

Salt and pepper to season

Place eggplant slices on a greased baking tray. Bake in the oven for 20 minutes at 200°C.

Heat oil in a frypan, add onion and garlic and sauté until onion is softened. Add tomatoes, tomato paste, oregano and seasoning and heat through. Combine spinach, ricotta, feta, parmesan, nutmeg, basil and seasoning. Combine eggs and cream. Layer a large square casserole dish with roasted eggplant, then tomato mixture, then spinach mixture, then pour over egg mixture. Top with grated tasty cheese. Bake at 180°C for 45 minutes or until well browned.

Total cooking time: 1 hour 10 minutes
Serves: 6

Frittata

Protein

1 tablespoon butter

2 leeks, sliced

6 mushrooms, sliced

1 red capsicum, seeded and diced

1 medium eggplant, peeled and diced

1 medium zucchini, diced

1 can of artichokes, quartered

2 cups of spinach

8 eggs

½ cup of sour cream

1 cup grated tasty cheese

In a large saucepan heat butter and sauté leeks and mushrooms for 3 minutes. Add capsicum, eggplant and zucchini and continue to stir-fry until cooked through. In a well-greased, round baking dish, scatter vegetables, artichokes and spinach; set aside. In a mixing bowl, whisk eggs until well beaten, add sour cream and cheese, mix well, pour over the vegetables. Bake in a moderate oven 40 minutes. Serve in slices on plates with blanched broccoli, yellow squash, beans and Creamy Lemon Mayonnaise.

Total cooking time: 60 minutes
Serves: 4

VEGETABLES AND LEGUMES

Vegetables and Legumes

Vegetable Curry

Chickpea Patties

Roasted Sweet Potato with Spicy Bean and Tomato Sauce

Grilled Haloumi and Vegetable Toss with Sweet Basil Pesto

Vegetable Kebabs

Roasted Tomato and Eggplant

Spicy Red Lentils and Tomatoes with Basmati Rice

Falafels

Fennel, Egg and Cheese Ramekins

Stuffed Eggplant with Basil and Chickpeas

Quick Napoli Sauce

Vegetables and Legumes

The following vegetables are suitable with carbohydrate and protein style meals: zucchini, tomato, celery, mushroom, eggplant, baby yellow squash, leek, onion, garlic, string beans, cucumber, broccoli, cauliflower, artichokes, french runner beans, string beans, bok choy, wombok, choy sum, capsicum, artichoke and lettuce

The following vegetables and legumes are suitable with carbohydrate meals only: sweet potato, peas, snow peas, lentils, yams, chickpeas, most legumes and mung beans.

The following vegetables and legumes should be avoided: potato, carrots, parsnip, beetroot, broad beans, pumpkin, swede and taro.

Vegetable Curry

Protein

1 tablespoon olive oil

1 large onion, chopped

2 cloves garlic, crushed

1 teaspoon fresh ginger, grated

1 tablespoon red curry paste

½ head cauliflower, cut into florets

½ head broccoli, cut into florets

3 baby eggplants, sliced

2 medium zucchinis, sliced

6 baby yellow squash, chopped

125g button mushrooms, peeled and halved

125g green string beans, trimmed and cut into
    10 cm lengths

4 tomatoes, diced

1 cup fresh coriander leaves, chopped

4 tablespoons sour cream

*Heat oil in a large saucepan, add onion, garlic, ginger and curry paste
and stir-fry 3 minutes or until onion has softened. Add cauliflower,
broccoli, eggplant, mushrooms, zucchini and yellow squash. Stir-fry
10 minutes or until vegetables are browned and cooked through.
Combine tomatoes and mushrooms with extra olive oil and stir-fry
5 minutes. Add sour cream, vegetables and coriander, heat through
and serve.*

Total cooking time: 35 minutes
Serves: 4-6

Chickpea Patties
Carbohydrate

1 red Spanish onion, finely chopped

2 cloves garlic, crushed

1 tablespoon ground cumin

2 cups cooked chickpeas

½ cup fresh coriander leaves, finely chopped

2 egg whites lightly beaten

⅔ cup dried low carbohydrate breadcrumbs

Salt and pepper to taste

Sauté onion and garlic. Combine all ingredients in a food processor until smooth. Form into patties and place on baking paper in the oven at 180°C for 30 minutes or until well browned and cooked through. Serve with chilli sauce and lettuce.

Total cooking time: 15 minutes preparation, 30 minutes cooking
Makes: 12 patties

Roasted Sweet Potato with Spicy Bean and Tomato Sauce

Carbohydrate

3 large sweet potatoes, scrubbed

1 large onion, chopped

2 cloves garlic, crushed

½ red chilli, seeded and chopped

2 teaspoons ground cumin

1 teaspoon ground coriander

6 large ripe tomatoes, diced

1½ cups cooked red kidney beans

1 tablespoon tomato paste (no added sugar)

1 lemon, juice

seasoning

½ cup fresh coriander leaves, chopped

Extra coriander to garnish

Bake whole sweet potatoes in oven for 1½ hours at 200°C. In a large saucepan, sauté onion and garlic in a little water for 3 minutes or until onion softens. Add spices and stir-fry a further minute. Add tomatoes, red kidney beans, tomato paste, lemon juice and seasoning. Simmer covered for 15 minutes. Remove lid and simmer a further 5 minutes or until sauce thickens. Stir through coriander and allow to cook a further 2 minutes. Remove sweet potato from the oven, halve and divide between six plates. Spoon over tomato and bean sauce. Garnish with extra coriander.

Total cooking time: 1 hour 30 minutes roasting, 20 minutes preparation
Serves: 6

Grilled Haloumi and Vegetable Toss with Sweet Basil Pesto
Protein

2 red capsicum, seeded and quartered

1 green capsicum, seeded and quartered

1 yellow capsicum, seeded and quartered

2 cups olive oil

3 cloves garlic, crushed

2 tablespoons fresh oregano, chopped

4 tablespoons fresh basil, chopped

1 teaspoon salt

1 teaspoon cracked black peppercorns

1 large eggplant, sliced lengthways, 1.5 cm slices

2 medium zucchinis, halved and sliced lengthways

2 red Spanish onions, ends intact, cut into wedges

220g jar artichoke hearts

220g haloumi, sliced into 1.5 cm thick slices

4 baby yellow squash, sliced

¾ cup semi-sundried tomatoes

2 cups fresh basil leaves, extra

2 cloves garlic, extra

5 tablespoons grated parmesan cheese

Place capsicum under a hot grill, skin side up, until skin blackens and blisters. Remove and place in a plastic bag to cool. Once cooled remove skin. Combine olive oil, garlic, oregano, basil and seasoning in a large container. Add capsicum, eggplant, onion, zucchini, haloumi, yellow squash and artichokes, plus marinade fluid from artichoke jar. Mix vegetables and haloumi well with the marinade fluid. Cover and refrigerate 12 hours. Once marinated, set capsicum, haloumi and artichokes aside. Place remaining vegetables on a baking tray and bake for 1½ hours at 120°C or until browned and cooked through.

Place marinated haloumi slices under a hot grill and brown both sides. In a food processor combine extra basil, extra garlic and parmesan cheese; mince well to form a paste.

In a large saucepan combine capsicum, roasted vegetables, haloumi, semi-sundried tomatoes, pesto and 2 tablespoons of the marinade fluid. Briefly stir-fry to heat through. Serve.

Total cooking time: 24 hours marinating, 1 hour 40 minutes cooking
Serves: 4 servings

Vegetable Kebabs

Carbohydrate

1 red capsicum, seeded and chunked

1 green capsicum, seeded and chunked

3 baby yellow squash, chunked

2 medium zucchini, 2 cm slices

2 red Spanish onions, ends intact, cut into wedges

220g tempeh, diced 2 cm pieces

15 button mushrooms, peeled and quartered

1 cup vegetable stock

2 cloves garlic, crushed

1 teaspoon fresh ginger, grated

1 small red chilli, seeded and chopped

1 tablespoon tomato paste (no added sugar)

1 lemon, juice and zest

Seasoning

Soak bamboo skewers in water for 12 hours to prevent them burning and charring. Thread vegetables and tempeh onto skewers. Place kebabs into a large sealable container Combine stock, garlic, ginger, chilli, tomato paste, lemon juice, zest and seasoning. Pour marinade over the kebabs. Allow kebabs to marinate overnight. Barbeque until well browned and cooked through.

Total cooking time: 24 hours soaking and marinating, 30 minutes cooking
Makes: approximately 32 kebabs

Roasted Tomato and Eggplant

Protein

4 medium eggplants, sliced lengthways, 1.5 cm thick

6 Roma tomatoes, sliced lengthways

½ cup olive oil

4 tablespoons fresh basil leaves, chopped

2 cloves garlic, crushed

Extra basil leaves

Salt and pepper to season

90g crumbled feta cheese

Basil to garnish

Arrange eggplant slices on a plate and sprinkle with salt. Allow to stand 30 minutes before rinsing. Pat dry. Combine olive oil, basil and garlic in a large container, add eggplant and tomato. Marinate at least 2 hours.

On a baking tray layer eggplant and tomatoes with extra basil leaves. Drizzle over some of the marinade fluid and season. Place in oven and bake at 250°C for 15 minutes. Crumble over feta cheese, return to oven for a further 5 minutes or until cheese is browned. Garnish with more fresh basil and drizzle over a little more of the marinade fluid and serve.

Total cooking time: 2 hours 30 minutes marinating, 30 minutes cooking
Serves: 4

Spicy Red Lentils and Tomatoes with Lemon and Herb Basmati Rice

Carbohydrate

2 onions, finely chopped

2 cloves garlic, crushed

1 teaspoon fresh ginger, grated

1 red chilli, chopped

1 teaspoon cardamom seeds

½ stick cinnamon

2 teaspoons turmeric

1 teaspoon garam masala

2½ cups dried red lentils

6 ripe tomatoes, diced

2 cups vegetable stock

1 tablespoon lemon juice

½ cup fresh coriander leaves, chopped

Salt and pepper to season

3 cups lemon and herb basmati rice

Heat a large saucepan, add 1 tablespoon of water and sauté onion, garlic ginger and chilli for 3 minutes. Add spices and fry for 1-2 minutes. Add lentils, tomatoes and stock, simmer covered for 20 minutes or until lentils soften. Stir through lemon juice coriander and seasoning; allow to simmer uncovered until all fluid has condensed before serving. Serve with Lemon and Herb Basmati Rice.

Total cooking time: 30 minutes
Serves: 6

Falafels

Carbohydrate

2 cans chickpeas, drained and rinsed

2 egg whites, lightly beaten

1 onion, finely chopped

½ cup *Performax*$_{TM}$ bread crumbs or equivalent

2 cloves garlic, crushed

4 tablespoons fresh parsley, finely chopped

4 tablespoons fresh coriander leaves, finely chopped

1 teaspoons ground garam masala

½ teaspoon cinnamon

Juice of ½ lemon

½ - 1 teaspoon Tabasco sauce

Salt and pepper to season

In a processor grind chickpeas finely. Add all other ingredients and process to form a rough paste. Form into balls and bake at 180°C for 30 minutes or until browned and cooked through. Serve warm or cold tossed through salsa, on top of mixed lettuce leaves or rice.

Total cooking time: 15 minutes preparation, 30 minutes cooking
Makes: approximately 30 falafels

Fennel, Eggplant and Cheese Ramekins

Protein

½ cup oil

2 zucchini, sliced on the diagonal

1 large eggplant, sliced

1 fennel bulb, sliced

1 onion, sliced

315g ricotta cheese

½ cup grated parmesan cheese

2 tablespoons fresh parsley, chopped

1 tablespoon fresh chives, chopped

1 red capsicum, seeded and quartered

1 yellow capsicum, seeded and quartered

1 tablespoon oil, extra

1 extra onion, finely chopped

2 cloves garlic, crushed

1 small red chilli, seeded and chopped

6 tomatoes

1 tablespoon tomato paste (no added sugar)

Extra parsley to garnish

Heat oil in a large frypan. Add zucchini, eggplant, fennel and onion and fry over high heat until beginning to brown. Set aside on paper to drain. In a mixing bowl combine ricotta, parmesan, parsley and chives.

Place capsicum under a grill, skin side up. Grill until skin becomes blackened and blistered. Remove from grill, place in a plastic bag and allow to cool. Once cooled remove skin.

Grease four ramekins and layer the vegetables, cheese mixture and capsicum. Ensure that a layer of fried eggplant is on the bottom and the top of the ramekin layers. Place ramekins in the oven at 200°C for 15 minutes.

Cut a cross into the bottom of each tomato. Drop individually into boiling water for 30 seconds. Peel and dice.

Heat extra oil in a saucepan, add onion and garlic and sauté 3 minutes or until onion softens. Add the chilli, tomatoes and tomato paste. Simmer until fluid condenses to form a sauce-like consistency. Remove sauce from the heat and puree in a food processor. Return to the heat and warm.

Turn out ramekins onto plates and pour sauce over top. Garnish with extra parsley.

Total cooking time: 40 minutes
Serves: 4

Stuffed Eggplant with Basil and Chickpeas
Carbohydrate

2 large eggplants

2 large ripe tomatoes

1 cup cooked basmati rice

1 medium zucchini, grated

1 medium onion, finely chopped

1 clove garlic, crushed

4 tablespoons fresh basil leaves, finely chopped

1 tablespoon fresh rosemary, finely chopped

1 tablespoon fresh marjoram, finely chopped

20 button mushrooms, peeled and sliced

1 cup cooked chickpeas

1 tablespoon lemon juice

Salt and pepper to season

Extra chopped basil to garnish

Halve eggplants lengthways. Scoop out flesh leaving 1 cm of flesh inside eggplant shells; reserve the scooped out flesh. Sprinkle eggplant shells with salt and allow to stand 20 minutes before rinsing and patting dry. Place eggplant shells on a baking tray and bake at 200°C for 15 minutes.

Meanwhile, sprinkle the eggplant flesh with salt, place in a colander in the sink and place a weighted plate on top, stand 2 hours before rinsing and patting dry. Chop eggplant finely.

Cut a cross into the bottom of each tomato and drop into boiling water for 30 seconds, peel and dice finely.

Sauté onion and garlic in a little water for 3 minutes. Add mushrooms and a little more water and stir-fry for another 3 minutes. To onion and mushroom mixture add eggplant flesh, tomatoes, rice, chickpeas, herbs, lemon juice and seasoning. Cook for 6 minutes or until mixture is hot. Spoon tomato and chickpea mixture into eggplant shells, enough to fill the shells but do not overfill. Return to the oven to bake for 15 minutes at 200°C. Serve on four plates with any remaining tomato and chickpea mixture. Garnish with fresh basil.

Total cooking time: 2 hours 30 minutes
Serves: 4

Quick Napoli Sauce
Carbohydrate/Protein

This recipe can be used as a sauce to pour over fresh pasta or dolmades.

1 large can of diced tomatoes (no added sugar)
1 medium brown onion
2 cloves of garlic
1 tablespoon tomato paste (no added sugar)
Salt and pepper
3 bay leaves

In a large non-stick fry pan, fry garlic and onions in a small amount of water until browned. Add tomatoes, tomato paste and bay leaves. Season with salt and pepper and allow to reduce on a low heat to form a sauce-like consistency.

Total cooking time: 10 minutes
Serves: 4 when poured over freshly cooked pasta.

PART 3

Now What?

CHAPTER 7

Frequently Asked Questions

What can I have on my cereal in the morning?

Soy milk is usually the best thing to use. One needs to read the information on the box first, and it is best to purchase the one with the lowest amount of sugar. You must try to find the 'malt free' variety. We have always bought Australia's Own malt free, for example. If you can't get this brand then you are looking for the one with the least amount of sugar per 100g. Less than 1g is best.

Can I drink alcohol?

Alcohol is by and large a bad carbohydrate. Even if you include red wine, which contains very little sugar, it becomes very difficult to lose weight. Sorry but you will need to swear off the booze while you are in the weight loss phase.

Can I eat fruit after my meal?

Fruit has a moderate glycemic index, and therefore can only be combined with other moderate carbohydrates. If you ate fruit at the end of a protein meal, namely one that contains fat, then as I have described earlier, that meal would become fattening as a result. The answer is: if you have a carbohydrate meal, you can include fruit, but with a protein meal you cannot. There is something quite unique about fruit. When you eat proteins the stomach becomes more acidic. When you eat carbohydrates the stomach becomes more alkaline. The funny thing about fruit is that it requires somewhere in between an acid and alkaline environment to be digested.

When you combine it with other foods it has the effect of disrupting the digestive process to some degree. That is why fruit is best eaten on an empty stomach. I normally eat fruit first thing in the morning, before eating the other carbohydrates that constitute my breakfast, like cereal for example. I then tend to forget about it for the rest of the day.

Are all fruits OK or should some be avoided?

Originally we included all fruits, but over time we have found that fruits like banana, watermelon and grapes are just too high in the GI and should be avoided. As for strawberries, rockmelon and kiwi fruit, just don't go overboard as they can affect your glycogen levels and cause you to plateau. When considering a certain fruit, check the GI in the tables at the back of the book or go to the Macquarie University website glycemicindex.com. The lower the GI the better and as with all the moderate carbs, just don't go overboard.

Why can't I have milk or yoghurt?

We originally included milk and yoghurt in the first version of *Low Carb Made Easy*, but we discovered that we were not getting the desired effect so we took it out. The only reason we could see was that the lactose, being a sugar, must pump up the glycogen in the liver. You are more than welcome to include it, but if you find that you are not losing weight then that could be why.

Can I have artificial sweeteners?

The answer is yes because the idea is that they do not cause insulin to be released. But artificial sweeteners are also bad for your health because they are often carcinogenic and addictive. So although they are OK from the view point of weight loss, they are not OK for your health. It's up to you.

Is it anything like the Atkins diet?

The two focus on carbs but the main difference is that the Atkins diet started up before the glycemic index and so doesn't use it. From discussion with patients who have tried both, the results are the same, but *Low Carb Made Easy* is certainly easier to apply and follow. The late Dr Atkins felt that the GI was a 'useful reference' but not much beyond that.

How long do I keep doing this?

Until you're happy with your weight. Then you can play around but you will find it difficult to go back to your old ways. Why? Because your body won't let you. It will know what 'sugar free', is all about after a while. So when you finally go for that treat you've been saving up for, prepare for disappointment. Of course you can keep eating the wrong foods but once your body has had the taste of real freedom it won't forget. That's why most people are very happy to go on with it so many years after reading the book. I find that folks simply prefer, more and more, to follow this way of eating. You will probably do likewise. As I said before, you can expect to lose about one kg per week, so the formula is: number of kg's equals number of weeks. Want to lose 8 kg? Then you have 8 weeks of 'no bad carbs'. Because you are only burning up fat, there's no risk of becoming skeletal and you can expect to reach a weight that is ideal for you. There is a point for every person when they're not carrying any extra weight: a lean mean 'grinning' machine, rather than a stick insect.

What do I do when I want a snack?

I find that if you eat a reasonable amount at each meal then the desire to snack disappears. However, you can have cheese as a snack, before or after a protein meal, or dried fruit before or after a carbohydrate meal. The only thing is that this will extend your 'time window', so you will have to take that into account. (Read the section on time windows again.)

Do I need to exercise?

Exercise is an essential part of daily activity, however it is not essential as far as this book goes. As you can see the only exercise you really need to do is to exercise proper judgement when deciding what to eat for each meal. One of the things that I always find unfortunate is seeing overweight people jogging to lose weight. 'If they only had a copy of the book,' I would often think, 'then the whole job would be so much easier'. (Cherie has actually had to caution me about hurling copies from the car window). The sad part is, that the person has already overtaxed themselves by not eating correctly, and now they are putting an even greater strain on their bodies by trying to burn it off.

With the GI, it is much easier to lose the weight first and then, as you get closer to your desired weight, begin getting into shape in the gym or on the track. After teaching Tai Chi for over ten years and almost twenty years of Martial arts, I am no stranger to daily exercise. The Chinese believe that anything that requires you to break into a light sweat is sufficient. If you are not into Tai Chi, then walking, swimming, Yoga or cycling are all good choices, and can be enjoyed regardless of your age.

Having said that, I have also met a great many people who have chosen to follow my book *and* go to the gym. What happens usually in this scenario is that the weight seems to come off quicker than 1 kg/week but it really depends on how much extra effort the person puts into it.

If this is the way you would like to go about it then 'more power to you', but unless there is some particular reason why you need it to come off faster, then the fact of the matter is, that you will achieve the same results, without the gym membership, eventually.

I've reached a plateau

I normally advise that eating more protein meals gets things going again. The explanation is a little complex but even when doing everything 'by the book' sometimes your body can still get some 'mileage' from the moderate carbs that you have been eating. Occasionally the glycogen in the liver can go from being empty to slowly getting topped up again. When this happens, your body switches back to the liver for the energy and not to the reserves on your hips and thighs. Eating protein has the effect of driving down the glycogen and restarting the weight loss. 'OK sit up straight, it's thinking cap time again.'

Another amazing thing that your body is capable of is getting energy from protein. Imagine if you couldn't get any carbs but could eat protein. Would you starve? No, because your body can convert protein into energy and this process is called **Ketogenesis**. Now what really is surprising is that it burns ketones more efficiently than it does cabohydrate. So why don't we just go around eating meat all day? Because if that's all you ate, and believe it or not there are some people out there who are trying to tell people to do exactly that, then eventually, after about three weeks, your blood becomes acidic.

Now we are getting to the extreme end of the spectrum, where 'low carb' has now become 'no carb'. If people are foolish enough to do this then it can eventually lead to damage of the kidneys and liver. This state is called **Ketoacidosis** and is highly undesirable and unnecessary. This point has been the basis for the confusion about 'low carb'. People with very little idea about the GI are suggesting that following a low carb diet leads to ketoacidosis. As we can plainly see, this couldn't be further from the truth. Let's face it, if 60% of people in the USA say it's the best diet they have been on and there's a population of about 330 million, then you do the maths. That's a lot of people who are getting great benefits. The reason why they are not dropping in the streets from kidney and liver failure is because their diets consist of cabohydrates *and* protein. If you turn to the recipe section in this book you will notice that practically every meal includes carbohydrate, some exclusively.

Including carbs with each meal is very different from eating meat for weeks on end, Funnily enough, I tried this when I was first learning about low carb and I found that I lasted for about two weeks before I gave up. I ate only meat and fat for the entire time and still lost weight (The only problem was the cave was starting to smell and my hands were sore from swinging the club.) Now you know more about it than the so-called experts do.

Going beyond this now, I have noticed that, from time to time, people will reach a plateau for no tangible reason. Every now and again it can just happen.

When someone is stubbornly staying on the same weight and refuses to budge, it can be for one of two reasons. It may be because they have reached an ideal weight and their body will not go any further. But more often than not, it is because they have missed some fundamental part of the infor- mation. As earlier stated, the rules are surprisingly rigid. It doesn't take much to slow the progress down. Sometimes it can be as simple as not observing the time intervals between the two types of meals, or maybe eating the wrong type of rice. Usually it is simply a matter of going over the basic details again to find the problem. A common piece of advice that I often give, is to try eating more of the protein meals for a while and see if this helps. Normally, eating more protein can kick start the process again.

What do I eat when I go out for a meal?

Just about every menu will include at least three dishes that you can choose from that fall within the guidelines. If this is not the case, it is very simple to have the kitchen omit one or two ingredients to make the meal OK. One technique for avoiding certain ingredients is to feign food allergies. A useful technique is to say something like 'Oh my doctor has told me that I am allergic to potato,' for example. People, for some reason, will not question expert advice on another person's health. This is usually enough to fob off unwanted attention and is a simple solution, rather than explaining that you are trying to follow a diet. This always requires some explanation, and the intricacies of knowledge such as this, can be lost on the uninitiated.

Will I ever be able to eat these types of foods again?

Realistically, you should forget about the things that are not good for you. Once you have a firm understanding of this knowledge, then the art of weight loss is yours. Should you find yourself eating those things that you know will make you put on weight, then you know the easiest way to lose it again.

I can't do it because ...

Pat Farmer is an Australian Ultra Marathon runner who, in the year 2000, ran right round the coast line of Australia, including Tasmania. To describe it as an incredible achievement would be an understatement. After arriving back in Sydney, he summarised with these words,

'When you really want to do something, in your heart of hearts, you will find a way, but if you don't want to do something, you will find an excuse.'

The people who have made remarkable change, to themselves and their lives, have put aside their excuses and 'found a way', to achieve their goals. When it really comes down to doing something, you end up just getting on with it. When you think back over your life, the times when you have achieved a personal milestone has always come with resolution and commitment. I thought Pat's words were worth mentioning, because at times I have to remind people to stop making excuses and just get on with it.

If this is so great, why hasn't my doctor or dietician heard about it?

Good question. As mentioned earlier a recent survey on abcnews.com asked 'Out of low calorie, low fat or low carb, which was the most successful diet?' Several thousand people responded and low carbo polled at around 60%, the highest response. So one could say that it is the most popular diet in the USA at the moment. The glycemic index has been around for more than twenty years, and low carbo recipes for the past five, so I often wonder why professional people still struggle to come to grips with it. Part of the reason, I believe, is that many would have to admit that they have been giving people the wrong information for many years, and you know what people are like when it comes to admitting they are wrong. I knew back in 1995, that the glycemic index was going to totally change the way we think about food, and I am glad to say that I was right. Every day I have people telling me how much weight they have lost, how their lives have changed, they feel better, haven't got a cholesterol problem etc. We are very glad that these changes are filtering out into the mainstream. More recently the GI value of some foods has been included on the packaging.

The wheels turn very slowly when it comes to social change, or as the Chinese would say: 'The ox is slow but the earth is patient'. So now for the big question!

CHAPTER 8

Now I have lost the weight, what do I do?

Wait! Should you be reading this section yet?

If the answer is no, then I suggest that you go back and don't try anything funny like that again! If not, then what are you waiting for?

I think first that congratulations are in order. You have successfully grasped this information, and the rest becomes simple. What happens now is that you need to be able to maintain your desired weight. Here is the low-down on how to do that.

As I said earlier, you can say goodbye to the bad carbohydrates. They only make you fatter. Well nothing's changed. What you can now do is to begin to combine the two types of meals. This means that you can start combining the carbohydrate menu with the protein menu. For example, you can now have Bolognaise Sauce with your pasta and you finally get to sprinkle Parmesan cheese on top at long last. You can also add meat to your rice dishes. Essentially, you can now jazz up the carbohydrate meal, and bring it more into line with regular cuisine. But before you go ballistic, I must hasten to add you must now try to keep fat down to a minimum when you are combining the moderate carbohydrates with meats and fats because if you get out of control, it's a slippery slope back to where you have come from.

As you know by now, the moderate carbohydrates can cause some insulin to be released. As a result this will most likely cause fat absorption. That is why, in this instance, fat has to be kept to a minimum. So such practices as trimming fat from meats, or draining excess fats and oils away from some dishes need to be done, but essentially you can afford to be more liberal with your cooking. If you find that you have 'pushed the envelope too far' and the new clothes are not as loose as before, then guess what? It's back to doing things 'strictly by the book' again. You will eventually become used to keeping your weight under control and compensating for any seasonal excesses (Xmas, Easter, Birthdays etc.) with ease.

Wine makes a comeback

As promised, wine can now be included with your meal. But before you embark on a week-long alcoholic bender, I must point out that most alcohols are still carbohydrate bomb shells, loaded with sugars that are just waiting to be absorbed. They will always make you put on weight. So watch out. If you must drink spirits, then my advice to you is first to be moderate and also to have the spirits straight up on the rocks whenever possible. Most mixed drinks are combined with sugar-enriched combinations, like dry ginger or cola. Incidentally, one spirit that has a zero GI is Scotch whisky, and, conveniently, the bottles are usually square shaped so they don't roll away from you when you're having 'a lie down'.

As far as beer goes, forget it. To an Australian that's going to hurt, but the bottom line is that beer contains a type of sugar called maltose. Maltose has a higher glycemic index than glucose, so the amount of sugar that is contained in this particular beverage is pretty much off the scale. Show me a regular beer drinker and I will show you a beer belly.

So what should you be drinking? Something that contains little sugar, and the answer is going to be wine. Let's face it, we have been drinking wine since Roman times. Wine is a good accompaniment to most meals (perhaps with the exception of breakfast, although if you had met some of my patients you'd wonder!) Here are some very good reasons why wine may be put on the table.

Heart specialists agree that wine helps in preventing heart disease. Red wine is a better choice, but fundamentally one can consume up to half a litre per day. That's right, half a litre! The number of people's faces I have seen light up at that remark is more than I can remember. More than half a litre is being excessive, and no longer becomes healthy, besides no one likes a lush. Red wine contains elements that can reduce cholesterol, and open the arteries and capillaries allowing blood to move more freely. This makes it easier for your heart to pump it around your body. If your heart doesn't need to work as hard, then obviously you can avoid having a heart attack with a little preventive medicine. The French, for example, include wine with most meals.

They also, as a people, enjoy very low levels of heart disease. Another reason why red wine is favourable is that it contains plenty of iron. This is because iron presses are used to crush the grapes, and the iron from them goes into the wine. As a result, red wine is a good source of iron too. It is also full of antioxidants.

Red wine has less residual sugar than white and becomes preferable, but not critical, to your choice. Here in Australia we are blessed with clean air and great soils and consequently we produce some of the finest wines in the world. This is lucky, because Australians are also the best drinkers in the world. (hic...good evening *drink*stable...I've been on a diet...hic!). Whatever you choose, moderation should still prevail.

Seasons

If you live in a part of the world that has four seasons, then you may recognise that there are periods during the course of the year when your weight increases and decreases. Normally during the warmer months one tends to lose a few kilos. For this there are a number of explanations. We tend to be more active and eat less for example. This is a time when we would like to enhance this already natural feature, and make sure that it happens as efficiently as possible. Conversely, in the colder months of the year, we are less active and tend to eat larger and stodgier meals. This is a time when the Chinese believe it's best to put on a little weight.

When patients approach me during the colder months with the view to losing weight, I always say it's OK to do so, but they will probably achieve better results in the warmer months and this is generally the case. Of course, when a person is greatly overweight, it doesn't matter what time of year it may be. The regime of weight loss must not be interrupted. But for those who have mastered this knowledge, controlling your weight becomes simple. During winter, if you want to, one can afford to loosen up a little and have the occasional bad food combinations. Let's be honest, a cold winter's night, a roast leg of lamb with a few roast potatoes, pumpkin and gravy and a bottle of red can be very enjoyable. Do it frequently enough and the scales will slowly creep up. The fun comes when it is time to shed those extra pounds.

Sometimes patients become panic stricken when they have not been careful enough and have gained weight. I happily assure them that they need only focus on the carbs again and the unwanted weight will come off like before. Feel free to experiment if you want. It will give you confidence and you will realise how well the *Low Carb Made Easy* formula works time and time again. Having said all that, it's true that the easiest way to get weight off in summer, is to keep it off during winter'. So please, all things in moderation, don't lose control. It is very easy to find yourself back where you started if you are not careful.

What does the future hold?

Over the years that I have eaten this way, I have allowed myself to ease and tighten the types of carbs that I eat in accordance with the seasons and sometimes with circumstance.

One thing that I have become acutely aware of is that, in the beginning, having something that wasn't strictly 'by the book', was a bit of a treat and as far as I was concerned it was always going to be that way.

However, as the years went by I became increasingly aware that these treats and occasional 'dinners' where I wasn't ordering, eventually became a pain in the backside, as my preference for low carb came to dominate and things that were going to have a negative effect on me were avoided. It's not simply about weight, as you will soon discover. Eating bad carb is not only bad for your health, it makes you feel like rubbish as well. Eventually you get tired of your excesses and whatever enjoyment you may have had is soon short lived as you are overtaken by the next day of feeling yuck.

I was surprised to discover that some of my original patients who started on low carb with me in the mid '90s all report similar experiences. So one could expect the same to be said for you dear reader. Sure you may go up and down with it, but over time you may eventually come to prefer it. Of this I am sure.

Conclusion

This knowledge is now yours and all within your grasp. The problem of controlling your weight and taking care of your health should never be a problem to you again, now that you have this understanding.

As the years go by, you will go from a beginner to what I like to think of as 'a black belt' when you finally become expert at using it. No matter what your age, you can follow this way.

By now you will be aware that there are many other good reasons why controlling your blood sugar level is desirable. As you explore this knowledge and become more familiar with it, the potential of what you have learnt will become clear. I hope you have enjoyed reading our book *Low Carb Made Easy*, and that the experience has brought you a more intimate understanding of your body and of yourself. Good luck and happy trails.

Yours in good health.

John Ratcliffe DipTCM, Grad Dip Psy

Tables and Appendices

Appendix A: Glycemic Index List

Next is a list of different carbohydrates as per the glycemic index. Be aware that I have included it because you can use it as a comparison, and for a 'gee wow I never realised' effect. The values are based on some 80 studies and are not definitive but rather a general guide.

The Bakery

Bulgar bread	53
Cake, angel food	67
Cake, banana, made with sugar	75
Cake, flan	65
Cake, pound	55
Cake, sponge	66
Croissant	67
Crumpet	69
Donut	76
Muffins	62
Pastry	59
Pita bread, white	57
Pizza, cheese	60
Semolina bread	64
Waffles	76

Beverages

Cordial, orange	66
Lucozade	95
Soft drink, Fanta	68
Soy milk	30

Breads

Bagel, white	72
Barley flour bread	67
French baguette	95
Hamburger bun	61
Kaiser roll	73
Linseed rye bread	55
Melba toast	70
Oat bran bread	48
Pumpernickel	50
Rye Kernel bread	46
Rye flour bread	55
Wheat bread, gluten free	90
Wheat bread, high fibre	68
Wheat bread, white	71
Wheat bread, wholemeal flour	69

Breakfast Cereals

All-bran	42
Breakfast bar	76
Coco pops	77
Cornflakes	83
Nutri-grain	66

Oat Bran	55
Porridge	61
Puffed Wheat	74
Rice Bran	19
Rice Bubbles	90
Shredded Wheat	70
Special K	64
Sultana Bran	72
Sustain	68
Toasted Muesli (commercial)	56
Wheat Biscuits	70

Cereal Grains

Barley	34
Buckwheat	55
Bulgar	48
Couscous	65
Cornmeal	69
Rice, Basmati	50
Rice, brown	65
Rice, Calrose	87
Rice, instant, boiled 1 min	46
Rice, instant, boiled 6 min	88
Rice, Sunbrown Quick	80
Rice, white	68
Rice, wild, Saskatchewan	57
Rye	34
Tapioca, boiled with milk	81
Wheat kernels	41

Biscuits

Arrowroot	77
Digestives	59
Oatmeal	55
Shredded Wheat	62
Shortbread	63
Wafers	77

Crackers

Breton Wheat Crackers	67
High Fibre Rye Crispbread	65
Jatz	55
Puffed Crispbread	81
Rice Cakes	77
Sao	70
Stoned Wheat Thins	67
Water Crackers	71

Dairy Foods

Ice cream	61
Ice cream, low fat	50
Milk, full fat	27
Milk, skim	32
Yoghurt low fat, fruit sugar sweet	33
Yoghurt, low fat, artificially sweet	14

Fruit and Fruit Products

Apple	39
Apple juice	40
Apricots	30
Banana	54
Cherries	22
Fruit salad	55
Grapefruit	25
Grapefruit juice	48
Grapes	46
Kiwifruit	52
Mango	56
Orange	44
Orange juice	51
Pawpaw	58
Peach, canned	46
Peach, fresh	42
Pear, canned	44
Pear, fresh	37
Pineapple	65
Pineapple juice	46
Plum	38
Raisins	63
Rockmelon	65
Sultanas	56
Watermelon	72

Legumes

Baked beans, canned	48
Beans, dried, not specified	28
Beans, dried, P. vulgaris	70
Black-eyed beans	42
Broad beans (fava beans)	78
Butter beans	31
Butter beans + 5g sucrose	43
Butter beans + 10g sucrose	44
Butter beans + 15g sucrose	77
Chickpeas (garbanzo beans)	32
Chickpeas, canned	42
Chickpeas, curry, canned	40
Haricot/navy beans	38
Kidney beans	29
Kidney beans, canned	51
Lentils, green	29
Lentils, green, canned	51
Lentils, not specified	28
Lentils, red	24
Lima beans, baby, frozen	31
Pinto beans	38
Pinto beans, canned	45
Romano beans	45
Soya beans	17
Soya beans, canned	14
Split peas, yellow, boiled	31

Pasta

Capellini	45
Fresh Fettuccine	32
Gnocchi	66
Instant noodles	48
Linguine	45
Macaroni	45
Macaroni and Cheese	64
Ravioli, durum, meat filled	39
Spaghetti, protein enriched	57
Spaghetti, white	59
Spaghetti, boiled 5 min	52
Spaghetti, durum	54
Spaghetti, wholemeal	53
Tortellini, cheese	51
Vermicelli	35
Rice pasta, brown	91

Vegetables

Beets	63
Carrots	70
French fries	75
Parsnips	98
Peas, dried	22
Peas, green	47
Potato, instant	82
Potato, baked	84
Potato, new	56
Potato, Pontiac, boiled	56

Potato, boiled, mashed	73
Potato, canned	62
Potato, white, not specified, boiled	56
Potato mashed	70
Potato, steamed	65
Potato, microwaved	82
Potato, white, Ontario	59
Pumpkin	76
Swede (rutabaga)	71
Sweet corn	55
Sweet potato	50
Yam	50

Snack foods and confectionery

Corn chips	73
Dark Chocolate	55
Jelly beans	80
Life Savers	70
Mars Bar	68
Muesli Bars	61
Popcorn	56
Potato crisps	54
Pretzels	80

Soups

Green pea soup, canned	66
Lentil soup, canned	43
Split pea soup	60
Tomato Soup	38

Sugars

Honey	73
Fructose	22
Glucose	100
Glucose tablets	102
High fructose corn syrup	63
Lactose	45
Maltodextrin	96
Maltose	110
Sucrose	65

Indigenous Foods

American Indian

Acorns stewed with venison	15
Cactus jam	91
Corn hominy	40
Corn tortilla w/desert ironwood	38
Fruit leather	70
Lima beans broth	35
Mesquite cakes	24
White teparies broth	30
Yellow teparies broth	28

South African

Brown beans	24
Gram dal (chana dal)	5
Maize meal porridge, unrefined	70
Maize meal porridge, refined	74
M'fino wild greens	68

Mexican

Black beans	29
Brown beans	38
Nopal prickly pear cactus	7

Asian Indian

Baisen(, chickpea flour)chapati	28
Bajra (millet)	58
Banana, unripe, steamed 1 hr.	70
Barley chapati	42
Bengal gram dal (chana dal)	12
Bengal gram dal with semolina	54
Black gram	43
Black gram dal with semolina	46
Green gram	38
Green gram dal with semolina	63
Horse gram	50
Jowar	77
Maize chapati	62
Ragi (or Raggi)	87
Rajmah (red kidney beans)	20
Semolina	66
Tapioca, steamed 1 hr.	70
Varagu	68

Australian Aboriginals

Bread (Acacia coriacea)	38
Bunya nut pine	47
Bush honey, sugar bag	43
Blackbean seed	7
Castanospermum australe	74
Cheeky yam	35
Macrozamia communis	42
Mulga seed (Acacia aneura)	7

Pacific Island Foods

Breadfruit	68
Sweet potato (Ipomoea batatas)	43
Taro	54

Chinese Foods

Rice vermicelli	58
Lungkow bean thread	26

Miscellaneous

Fish fingers	38
Sausages	28
Sustagen Hospital Formula	42
Tofu frozen desert, non-dairy	112
Ultracal	38
Vitari	28

As you can see, a lot of carbohydrates raise your blood sugar level over the limit, but, conversely, there are still quite a few that are parts of an everyday diet. I find it interesting that a lot of the indigenous foods have a very low glycemic index.

NB. Some of the foods need explanation, like fish fingers, for example, with a GI of 40. I wouldn't advise going out and living off a diet of fish fingers because of it. When you combine fat with carbohydrates, the fat causes the body to take longer to absorb the food, so the rise in the blood sugar will be lower. However 40 still makes it moderate so the fat would be absorbed.

If you want to try including something that you believe has a low GI, give it a go, but if you find that you are no longer losing weight or even gaining weight then I would advise taking it out again. The combinations that we suggest are the culmination of experience but are by no means exhaustive. We know that the formula works when followed correctly.

Appendix B: Glycemic Loading

Glycemic Loading (GL) is something that you might come across when you look deeper into low carb. It comes from research done at Harvard University in the United States. Their argument is that a better indication of insulin response can be found by taking the amount of carbohydrate that is actually contained in a certain carb and multiplying it by its GI and then dividing by 100.

So using carrot as an example: Its GI is 70, but it only contains 5g of carbohydrate per serve (1 serve = 30g) so the GL would be: 70 × 5 = 350, divided by 100 = 3.5 rounded up to 4. So carrot despite having a high GI, has a low GL of 4. So should be OK to eat. To use another example using the same formula on a crumpet (GI 69 and 19g of carbohydrate) we get; 69 × 19 divided by 100 = 13 and so on.

The argument put forward by the team at Harvard is that people should be more concerned with the *amount* of carbohydrate that they are eating rather than the GI, so a person may say 'OK today my *cumulative* total of carbohydrate will be no more than a GL100'. So using the above examples, that's the equivalent of 6 crumpets and 10 serves of carrot for the day.

According to the boffins, this would be alright. Now I realise that it may sound like I'm being unfair with my crumpet analogy, but it doesn't really matter because you can use any carb you want. It's all about the *amount* of that carb that you consume. Now GL is actually quite good in some ways because I have known for many years that if a patient goes overboard on moderate carbs, it can stop them from losing weight. So we caution people not to eat too much of the moderate carbs. What's too much?

For example, a patient contacts us and says 'I'm not losing any weight' and we always ask 'what are you eating?' When they get to the part about the bowl of strawberries for breakfast or the packet of dried apricots at lunch time or the three bowls of rice and sweet potato for dinner, we pretty much know that we have found the reason. Just off the point for a moment. When people tell us this, we also know that they have only just started following the book, because it's common for people to want to overcompensate for the lack of sugar and this is how they do it. It soon passes.

Now the GL offers another angle and tells us that amount does matter and from the above example I agree. It helps me understand why we can eat some carbs that push the GI envelope and still lose weight as long as it's in moderation. However the study also shows that a normal daily intake would be around 100 or so. The first problem is, what if we want to lose weight when using the GL? For arguments sake, let's say we reduce the daily GL intake by half to 50. Then we are talking about the daily carb intake that would be 6 apples or 10 serves of carrot or 5 kiwi fruits or 2½ serves of rice or pasta or potato or cornflakes.

Obviously if the only carbs you were eating was 6 apples a day then, I would be expect that you'd see some results but 10 serves of carrot! I know that this will stop you dead in your tracks. The other problem is that there is no mention of protein and fats. What if you were combining fat with these carbs? Of course it would be absorbed. So how does that help people look after their health? Another concern is that some people will reach the conclusion that cutting carbs out completely is the logical step to be sure of good results and, as I have mentioned earlier we have actually heard of people being encouraging to do just that. Naturally this leads to problems like ketoacidosis.

My spin on this debate is this: the GI is huge and there's no denying that it's having an enormous impact on many things. The Harvard study, although correct, in real terms doesn't overshadow the relevance of the GI. I'm sure that the fellows at Harvard would completely disagree with me on this and in fact I am certain of it, because I think that this is really a battle to claw back the high ground that the GI has already taken in the scientific world. The reason that I say this is that part of the long road to acceptance is the poo- pooing that new ideas get along the way. Different institution will try to be 'more right' than others.

Regrettably, it's the general public who get confused by the conflicting information. So the reason we don't use the GL, beside making things more complicated is that fortunately we don't rely solely on lab result to tell us what to eat. Some things we also know from experience.

Appendix C: Metabolic Syndrome aka Syndrome X

This is something else you may stumble upon in your studies. Metabolic Syndrome or Syndrome X was first noticed in 1988. It is a collection of symptoms that came to be first known as Syndrome X, then was referred to as Metabolic Syndrome. The WHO already has an MS and didn't like the sound of SX, so now wants it to be referred to as Insulin Resistance Syndrome (IRS).

Basically, this is a condition where the person has abnormally high BSL and insulin in the blood all the time. The problem is that the insulin isn't doing anything to get rid of the glucose. This is commonly seen in obese or over-weight people who also present with high cholesterol and triglycerides levels and hypertension (high blood pressure). Allow me to digress for a moment. Let's face it, if you have all of the above symptoms, then your health isn't going to be too good anyway.

What researchers believe is that the reason for this condition is that the person has had a high exposure to insulin for a long time and the cells have become resistant, stopping the excess glucose in the blood from being absorbed. They believe that IRS is a precursor to type II diabetes, although observations show that people can have this condition for several years without going on to develop diabetes. Researchers believe that weight gain, hereditary factors, sedentary life-styles, overeating and age may also be related. If you can put two and two together, you can understand why people would develop this and also quite possibly how to treat it.

Appendix D: Glossary

Bok Choy: *Chinese green leafy vegetable similar to spinach*

Capsicum: *red, green or yellow pepper*

Chickpeas: *garbanzo beans*

Choy Sum: *Chinese broccoli*

Coriander: *cilantro*

Eggplant: *aubergine*

Fennel bulb: *bulb-like white vegetable, smells like aniseed*

Flat-leaf parsley: *Italian parsley*

Haloumi: *Greek style cheese*

Prawns: *shrimp*

Saffron threads: *Indian spice*

Spring onion: *scallion, shallot*

Tamarind: *made from the fruit of the tamarind tree*

Zucchini: *courgette*

Appendix E: Conversion Table

Weights

Dry

Metric	Imperial
30g	1oz
60g	2oz
90g	3oz
100g	3½oz
125g	4oz
150g	5oz
185g	6oz
200g	7oz
250g	8oz
280g	9oz
315g	10oz
330g	11oz
370g	12oz
400g	13oz
440g	14oz
470g	15oz
500g	16oz (1lb)
750g	24oz (1½ lb)
1kg	32oz (2lb)

Liquids

Metric	Imperial
30ml	1 fl oz
60ml	2 fl oz
90ml	3 fl oz
100ml	3½ fl oz
125ml	4 fl oz
150ml	5 fl oz
190ml	6 fl oz
250ml	8 fl oz
300ml	10 fl oz
500ml	16 fl oz
600ml	20 fl oz (1 pint)
1 litre	32 fl oz

Cooking temperatures

	Celsius	Fahrenheit
very slow	120	250
slow	150	300
moderately slow	160	315
moderate	180	350
moderately hot	200	400
hot	220	425
very hot	240	475

Bibliography

Among the literally hundreds of studies of the Glycemic Index in scientific literature, these are some of the more important and most recent. But be warned, some of the G.I. values can vary from study to study.

1. Ahern, J.A., et al. "Exaggerated hyperglycemia after a pizza meal in well-controlled diabetics." Diabetes Care, Vol 16, April 1993, pp. 578-80.

2. Allen, Ann de Wees, "Edible Computer Chips Chart of Glycemically Acceptible Foods 1995-1996," and "Edible Computer Chips Chart of Glycemically Unacceptible Foods 1995-1996," pages 38-50 in Diabetes Care: Control for Life. Diabetes Resource Center Inc., Winter Haven, Florida, 1996.

3. Arnot, Robert. Dr. Bob Arnot's Revolutionary Weight Control Program.

4. Bahan, Deanie Comeaux. Sugarfree New Orleans: A Cookbook Based on the Glycemic Index.

5. Buchhorn, Des. "Adjusted carbohydrate exchange: food exchanges for diabetes management correctedwith the glycaemic index." Australian Journal of Nutrition and Dietetics, Volume 54, 1997, pp. 65-68.

6. Foster-Powell, Kaye, Jennie Brand Miller and Stephen Colagiuri. Pocket Guide to the G.I. Factor for People with Diabetes.

7. Gittleman, Ann Louise. Get the Sugar Out: 501 Simple Ways to Cut the Sugar Out of Any Diet.

8. Hermansen, K., et al. "Influence of ripeness of banana on the blood glucose and insulin response in type 2 diabetic subjects." Diabetic Medicine, Vol. 9, October 1992, pp. 739-43.

9. Heaton, Kenneth W. et al. "Particle size of wheat, maise, and oat test meals: effects on plasma glucose and insulin responses and on the rate of starch digestion in vitro." The American Journal of Clinical Nutrition, Vol. 47, 1988, pp. 675-682.

10. Holt, Susanne H.A., Janette C. Brand Miller, and Peter Petocz. "An insulin index of foods: the insulin demand generated by 1000-kJ portions of common foods." The American Journal of Clinical Nutrition, Vol. 66, 1997, pp. 1264-76.

11. Jenkins, David J.A., et al. "Glycemic Index of Foods: a Physiological Basis for Carbohydrate Exchange." The American Journal of Clinical Nutrition, Vol. 34, March 1981, pp. 362-366. The initial glycemic index research. A classic.

12. Jenkins, D.J.A. and Jenkins, A.L. "Treatment of hypertriglyceridemia and diabetes." Journal of the American College of Nutrition, Vol 6, 1987, pp.11-17.

13. Jenkins, David J.A. et al. "Starchy Foods and Glycemic Index." Diabetes Care, Vol. 11, No. 2, February 1988, pp. 149-159.

14. Lipetz, Philip. The Good Calorie Diet. Harper Spotlight paperback, 1994.

15. Lipetz, Philip, and Monika Pichler. Naturally Slim and Powerful. Andrews and McMeel, 1997.

16. Miller, Janette Brand. "International tables of glycemic index." The American Journal of Clinical Nutrition, Vol. 62 (supplement), 1995, pp. 871S-893S. The first comprehensive listing of glycemic index results, containing almost all foods listed in Professor Brand Miller's 1996 book.

17. Miller, Janette Brand, et al. "Rice: a High or Low Glycemic Index Food?" The American Journal of Clinical Nutrition, Vol. 56, 1992, pp. 1034-1036.

18. Miller, Jennie Brand, Kaye Foster-Powel, and Stephen Colagiuri. The G.I. Factor: The Glycaemic Index Solution. Sydney: Hodder Headline, 1996.

19. Montignac, Michel. Dine Out & Lose Weight: The French Way To Culinary Savior Vivre. Montignac U.S.A. Inc., 1995. 298 paperback pages

20. National Diabetes Information Clearinghouse, a Service of the National Institute of Diabetes and Digestive and Kidney Diseases, National Institutes of Health. Diabetes and the Glycemic Index Information Packet. March 1996, 9 pages. While the U.S. Government does not endorse the glycemic index, this information packet certainly shows that it recognizes the concept. The packet consists of two articles:

21. Dinsmoor, Robert S. "The Glycemic Index," Diabetes Self-Management, Winter 1984-85, pages 22-24. A very early popularization of the work of Dr. David Jenkins, who developed the glycemic index concept in 1981.

22. Brand Miller, Janette C. "Importance of glycemic index in diabetes" American Journal of Clinical Nutrition , Vol. 59 (supplement), 1994, pp. 747S-752S. A comprehensive and professional review of the literature.

23. Paice, Derek A. Diabetes and Diet: A Type 2 Patient's Efforts at Control. Paice & Associates Inc.

24. Podell, Richard N., and William Proctor. The G-Index Diet. Warner-Books, Inc., 1993.

25. Salmerón, Jorge, et al. "Dietary Fiber, Glycemic Load, and Risk of Non-insulin-dependent Diabetes Mellitus in Women." The Journal of the American Medical Association, Vol. 277, February 12, 1997, pp.472-477.

293

26. Smith, Ulf. "Carbohydrates, Fat, and Insulin Action." The American Journal of Clinical nutrition, Vol. 59 (supplement), 1994, pp. 686S-689S.

27. Steward, H. Leighton et al. Sugar Busters! Cut Sugar to Trim Fat. New York: Ballantine Books, 1998,

28. Thomas, D.E., Brotherhood, J.R., and Brand, J.C. "Carbohydrate feeding before exercise: effect of the glycemic index." International Journal of Sports Medicine, Vol 12, 1991, pp.180-186.

29. Trout, D.L., Behall, K.M., and Osilesi, O. "Prediction of glycaemic index for starchy foods." The American Journal of Clinical Nutrition, Vol. 58, 1993, pp. 873-8.

30. Wahlqvist, M.L. (Department of Medicine, Monash University, Monash Medical Centre, Clayton, VIC.,Australia). "Nutrition and diabetes." Australian Family Physician, Vol 26, April 1997, pages 384-389.

31. Whitaker, Julian. "My Latest Thinking on Diet: All Carbohydrates Are Not Created Equal

32. Wolever, Thomas M.S. et al. "The Glycemic Index: Methodology and Clinical Implications." The American Medical Journal

33. Journal of Clinical Nutrition, Vol. 54, 1991, pp. 846- 854.

34. Wolever, Thomas M.S. et al. "Glycemic Index of Fruits and Fruit Products in Patients with Diabetes." The International Journal of Food Sciences and Nutrition, Vol. 43, 1993, pp.205-212.

The Glycemic Index Elsewhere on the Internet

1. A recent review of the literature on the glycemic index is a paper by Maria Kalergis, MSc RD, Danièle Pacaud, MD, Jean-François Yale, MD, "Attempts to Control the Glycemic Response to Carbohydrate in Diabetes Mellitus: Overview and Practical Implications" in the Canadian Journal of Diabetes Care22(1):20-29, 1998. This long paper is on-line at the Medscape site at: http://www.medscape.com/CDA/CJDC/1998/v22.n01/dc2201.02.kale/dc2201.02.kale- 01.html

2. The most scientific background on the glycemic index on the Web is "Carbohydrates in Human Nutrition; Interim Report of a Joint FAO/WHO Expert Consultation, Rome, Italy, 14 to 18 April 1997." This report by an international committee of carbohydrate experts assembled by the United Nations reports on the current scientific knowledge of carbohydrates, which turns out to be much more complex than a someone like myself has ever dreamed possible. It also contains a valuable section on the glycemic index itself, "The Role of the Glycemic Index in Food Choice." The URL is http://www.fao.org/waicent/faoinfo/economic/esn/carbohyd/carbohyd.htm

3. The most extensive popular discussion of the glycemic index on the Web is the "Official Ann de Wees Allen Web Site." It includes pages on the The Glycemic Index and The Glycemic Research Institute, which is a nonprofit organization based in Washington, D.C., which Ann deWees Allen, N.D., heads as its senior research scientist. The URL is http://www.anndeweesallen.com/

4. You can receive a long e-mail, "Americans are Getting Fatter and Fatter: The Glycemic Connection," by Ann de Wees Allen, N.D., by sending a message to index@adds2u.com. The message needs no subject nor anything in the body. The response you will receive includes her chart of glycemically acceptable and unacceptable foods.

5. "Sugars, Insulin, Appetite and Body Fat: The Glycemic Index Connection" contains a table of the glycemic indexes of about 50 foods. Unfortunately, the base is not stated (it is, in fact, glucose = 100), and is based almost entirely on just one study (Jenkins, 1981), ignoring about 80 studies since then. Worse, not every glycemic index can be sourced to any professional study. The URL is
http://www.smartbasic.com/glos.news/3glyc.indx.dec93.html

6. "The Glycemic Index" is a different Web page, but has the same limitations as the one above. Its URL is http://www.diabetesnet.com/gi.html

7. Lisa A. Piguet in Los Altos Hills, California, has a "Glycemic index of some carbohydrates," about 39 of them with the base glucose = 100 at http://www.best.com/~piguet/glycemic-index.html

8   Nancy Cooper, R.D., C.D.E., a diabetes nutrition specialist at the International Diabetes Center in Minneapolis has a short, rather negative, Q&A about the glycemic index reprinted from the March/April 1997 issue of Diabetes Self-Management. The URL is http://www.diabetes-self-mgmt.com/ma97que.html

9. The Montignac Universal Web site has a short "Glycaemic Index Table" based on glucose = 100 at http://www.montignac.com/en/gindex.html

10. Marcel Bovy in Amsterdam, Holland, has a fine review of the diet method developed by Michel Montignac, which makes considerable use of the glycemic index. The URL is http://www.geocities.com/HotSprings/4582/

11. "The Glycemic Index; How quickly do foods raise your blood sugar?" is an attractively presented page on the Diabetes Mall. The URL is http://www.diabetesnet.com/gi.html

12. Glycemic Index of Selected Foods is a short list of about 20 foods. The unstated reference food is glucose.The URL is http://www.sugarbusters.com/food.html

13. "Timed-Release Glucose: Nutritional Management of Hypoglycemia" by Drs. Stacey J. Bell and R. Armour Forse is a careful, professional explanation of the glycemic index in support of two food products -NiteBite and Zbar — designed with use of the principles behind the glycemic index. The URL is http://www.nitebite.com/nutrition_full.htm

14. "The Glycemic Index & Weight Loss" is a Web site in support of the Sugar Busters! diet. The URL is http://busycooks.miningco.com/library/features/blgiindex.htm

15. "The Glycemic Index" by Peter Schroeter is a comprehensive site. Particularly valuable is his experiment on mixed meals. The URL is http://silcom.com/~shushin/glycemic/glycemic.html

16. "The Glycemic Index & Weight Loss" is a decent summary of the glycemic index on Lynn Nelson 's "Mining Co. Guide to Busy Cooks." The URL is http://busycooks.tqn.com/library/features/blgilists.htm

17. The resource that we use when someone throws a curly question at us like what is the GI of 'Yak milk yoghurt' or 'Sun dried bees knees' is this web site by Macquarie Uni. The URL is http://www.glycemicindex.com

Recipe Index

A Antipasto 131

Asparagus and salmon with hollandaise sauce 169

Asian style spicy mince in lettuce cups 196

B Baba ghanoush 121

Bacon and onion dip 124

Bacon, cabbage and cauliflower soup 148

Baked ricotta with semi-dried tomatoes 174

Baked spinach flan 234

Barley pilau 176

Basmati rice salad 152

Beverages 91

Blanched green vegetables with light vinaigrette 171

Bok choy and tofu soup 146

Bread 97

Broccoli and cauliflower alfredo 167

C Cabbage noodles 168

Cajun seafood with vegetables 222

Cauliflower and cream cheese soup 134

Cheese and sliced meats 128

Chicken and mushrooms with mustard dressing 194

Chicken and prosciutto with creamy cheese sauce 186

Chicken cacciatore 184

Chicken, parmesan and spinach loaf 192

Chicken with fennel and feta cheese 188

Chicken stock 109

Chickpea patties 240

Chickpeas and rice 177

Chilli sauce 119

Cinnamon bulgur with fresh fruit 96

Coleslaw with coriander and chilli 165

Cordon bleu meat balls 209

Creamy mushroom soup 143

Creamy asparagus soup 138

Creamy lemon mayonnaise 116

Curried cream of chicken soup 144

Curried octopus with tomatoes and tamarind 217

Curried veal and vegetables 206

D *Dolmades* 130

E *Easy bacon and cheese omelette* 228

Easy beef stroganoff 204

Egg and zucchini hash browns 231

Eggplant and leek soup 147

F *Falafels* 247

Fennel, eggplant and cheese ramekins 248

Fish and red capsicum terrine 221

Fish stock 110

Fresh prawn curry with lemon myrtle 219

Fresh tomato soup with chickpeas and rosemary 135

Fresh vegetables 129

Fried whitebait with lemon and mustard dressing 225

Frittata 236

Fruit salad 95

G *Garlic prawns with creamy cheese sauce* 223

Greek style fish 214

Green curry chicken 193

Green curry paste 114

*Grilled haloumi and vegetable toss with sweet basil
and pesto* 242

H   *Hearty vegetable soup 142*

Hollandaise sauce 117

Hot roast chicken with herbed stuffing 189

Hummus 122

I   *Indian style red lentil pilau 178*

Indian style vegetables 166

K   *Kangaroo with leeks and lemon dressing 202*

L   *Lamb and artichoke kebabs 208*

Lamb masaman curry casserole 198

Lemon and herb basmati rice 172

Light vinaigrette with fresh parsley and roasted garlic 118

M   *Marinated feta cheese and mushrooms 170*

Marinated haloumi with roma tomatoes and spinach 152

Meat loaf with blue cheese sauce 199

Mediterranean lamb stir-fry 197

Mexican capsicum and bean salad 153

Masaman curry paste 113

Muesli 101

O   *Original tomato soup 145*

P   *Pesto 115*

Poached eggs on spinach with garlic sauce 106

Porridge 105

Prosciutto roll-ups 127

Q   *Quick napoli sauce 252*

R   *Raita 120*

Red curry paste 111

Risotto with fresh dill and roasted tomato wedges 182

Roma tomatoes with haloumi and prosciutto served with garlic mushrooms and crispy bacon 102

Roasted chickpeas 126

R   *Roasted ocean trout with wasabi dressing and nori crisps 218*

Roasted sweet potato with spicy beans and tomato sauce 241

Roasted tomato and eggplant 245

Roasted vegetable salad with salsa 155

*Roast lamb and vegetables with creamy cheese sauce
    and pesto   200*

S   *Salmon, dill and mascapone muffins with creamy lemon
    mayonnaise 216*

Salmon dip 123

Salmon with leeks and oyster mushrooms 226

Salsa 114

Salsa cheesecake 230

Schnitzel 200

Seafood chowder 136

Semi sun-dried tomatoes 129

Spicy barbeque chicken 185

Spicy egg roll-ups 232

Spicy fish cakes with vietnamese style dressing 220

Spicy mince burgers with salsa 212

*Spicy red lentils and tomatoes with lemon and herbed
    basmati rice 246*

Spicy roasted chickpeas 126

Spicy roasted vegetable paella with chickpeas 180

Squid and octopus salad 160

Steamed ginger chicken with asian greens 190

Stir-fried chinese vegetables 164

Stuffed eggs 132

Stuffed eggplant with basil and chickpeas 250

Stuffed lamb fillets with grilled vegetables and pesto 205

Sweet potato and lentil soup with coriander 139

T   *Tabouli 173*

Toast 100

Traditional caesar salad 156

Tuna and vegetable salad 162

Turkish tabouli salad with red lentils 151

V   *Vegetable crisps 127*

Vegetable curry 239

Vegetable kebabs 244

Vegetable stock 108

Vegetables and legumes 238

Vietnamese style barramundi 224

Vietnamese style spicy seafood soup 140

W   *Warm asparagus and egg salad with hollandaise sauce 229*

Warm red curry chicken salad with salsa verde 150

Warm thai beef salad 158

Z   *Zucchini and cheese omelette with mushrooms in a creamy sauce 104*

Index

A

Acidophilus 68
Alcohol 255
Anaerobic bacteria 65–66
Artificial sweeteners 257
Atkin's diet 257

B

Bad carbs 33–35, 58
Basmati rice 37
Binge eating 70–72
Bloating 66
Blood sugar 17–32
Bread addiction 53–55

C

Caffeine 51
Calcium 46
Candida 66–67
Carbohydrates 18, 20–21, 26,
    30–36, 39–40
Carbo lipids 45–46
Chinese medicine 10, 67
Cholesterol 64–65

D

Dairy 46, 257
Diabetes 11, 21, 57–60, 63
Dietician 263
Digestion 65–68

E

Energy 24, 61, 75
Exercise 258–259

F

Fats 19, 30, 266
Frequently asked questions
    255–264
Fructose 38
Fruit 73–74, 256

G

Glucose 23–26
Glycemic Index 21–23, 27,
    274–285
Glycemic loading 286–288

H

Heart disease 64–65
Hypoglycemia 57–60

I

Insulin 17–32, 63–65, 69–72,

K

Ketones 260
Ketoacidosis 260–261
Ketogenesis 260

L

Lactose 257
Lipids 36, 47
Liver 23, 260

M

Maltose 66
Meal Planner 81–88
Metabolic syndrome 289
Metabolism 75

N
Nuts 45

O
Obesity 25, 62
Oils 19

P
Pancreas 29, 58–59
Pasta 37
Polycystic Ovarian Syndrome
    69–70
Protein 18, 30, 36, 42–44
Pure rye bread 38, 53

R
Recipes 89–252
Rules 76–77

S
Scales 76
Snacks 258

Soy milk 52, 255
Sugar craving 18, 73–74
Syndrome X 289

T
Tai Chi 259
Time windows 46–48, 258

U
Ultra marathon 263

W
Weight loss 17–32, 38, 76, 259
Wine 266–288
World Health Organisation 17, 62

Y
Yoghurt 68

Z
Zero fat 40

Low Carb Made Easy

Please visit the *Low Carb Made Easy* website for all inquiries, updates, new recipes, and support services. Inquiries may also be made through the contact details outlined below.

Better Healing Solutions
PO Box 5207
Burnley, Vic, 3121
Australia
Ph: 1300 137 014

www.low-carbohydrate.com